Quarterly Essay

CONTENTS

Quarterly Essay is published four times a year by Black Inc., an imprint of Schwartz Publishing Pty Ltd. Publisher: Morry Schwartz.

ISBN 186-395-286-1 ISSN 1832-0953

ALL RIGHTS RESERVED.
No part of this publication may be reproduced, stored in a retrieval system, or transmitted in any form by any means electronic, mechanical, photocopying, recording or otherwise without the prior consent of the publishers.

Essay & correspondence © retained by the authors.

Subscriptions (4 issues): $49 a year within Australia incl. GST (Institutional subs. $59). Outside Australia $79. Payment may be made by Mastercard, Visa or Bankcard, or by cheque made out to Schwartz Publishing. Payment includes postage and handling.

To subscribe, fill out and post the subscription card, or subscribe online at:

www.quarterlyessay.com

Correspondence and subscriptions should be addressed to the Editor at:

Black Inc.
Level 5, 289 Flinders Lane
Melbourne VIC 3000 Australia
Phone: 61 3 9654 2000
Fax: 61 3 9654 2290
Email:
quarterlyessay@blackincbooks.com (editorial)
subscribe@blackincbooks.com (subscriptions)

Editor: Chris Feik
Management: Sophy Williams
Production Co-ordinator: Caitlin Yates
Publicity: Anna Lensky
Design: Guy Mirabella
Printer: Griffin Press

PREFACE

It's a mysterious business, the way we end up being certain kinds of persons, pursuing certain kinds of interests. Such complex tangles of chance and fate which, as they say, is character.

I was a visiting scholar at Cambridge University recently, where this puzzle was brought home to me during my first high-table supper. On my right was a rather shy man whose "field" was "margins".

We might have left it at that, had I not, with saving inspiration, realised how interesting the study of margins might be – illuminated manuscripts! annotations!

"No," he said. "Just ... ordinary margins."

I turned to the man on my left, who was from Sweden. His field of study boiled down to female urine.

I turned back to the man on my right. His was an esoteric branch of the study of the history of books, and he didn't study anything that might occur within the margins of books, but simply the margins themselves – the empty bits.

I kept refilling his glass, and by the time coffee came around, he had quite come out of his shell. While the man on my left was entertaining the table with stories of Swedish tankers shipping vats of female urine to the States for the production of HRT, I asked my new friend why he felt drawn to the study of margins. He stared deeply into his wineglass, and replied, "I've never given it any thought, but I suppose it might be because I am a marginal person."

Quite so. And I study nomadism because I am a nomadic person. That is the first of my credentials for writing this essay – an inclination to speculate upon the human impulse to wander. The origin of my own peripateticism is difficult to pinpoint, but once you are on a certain trajectory, the world colludes to keep you on it. Reality takes on the shape of a fishtrap and if you are not constantly vigilant, down the funnel you go. At the end of which, you might find yourself being described as a "specialist".

I am not a specialist. I've never been trained to focus down to that one piece of mosaic to add to the ever-extending wall of human knowledge. I am a writer, and a writer's sensibility is different. More magpie-like, picking up bits of mosaic here and there, to fit into a pattern of one's own.

The other credential is that I have visited, lived or travelled with "traditional" nomads in various parts of the world, on and off, for thirty years.

But even before I begin, I find myself stalled by the requirements of exactitude, and must resort to inverted commas.

The idea of the "traditional" as something quite static, with a recognisable boundary, something antithetical to (and victim of) the modern, has been unstitched by contemporary discourse. The social sciences now recognise that physical and definitional boundaries are flexible and porous, that cultures, tribes, societies, have always been changing, interacting with neighbours and adapting to new circumstances. With the advent of globalisation — the pervasive spread of cultural products and practices — this flux is dramatically faster and more apparent. But that is a quantitative difference, not a qualitative one.

No longer can the "ethnographic subject" occupy a bounded geographical space — a system unto itself. That was a concept that old-fashioned anthropology imposed. A useful story which, however, was not empirically correct. These days anthropologists are more likely to investigate borderlands and to analyse flow than to study an illusory fixity. They focus on processes, not essences.

Which no doubt is as it should be, but leaves the problem of language unsolved. How to give definition to things that are essentially fugitive? Would it clarify matters if instead of the word "traditional", I substituted "residual"? Or "classical"? Not really. So what do I mean, exactly, by "traditional nomadism"?

For the purposes of this essay, I mean: fairly frequent, sometimes seasonal physical movement, combined with an economy based on hunting, gathering and/or fishing; pastoralism; artisanship; service or trade. It is a strategy permitting access to resources and encouraging particular kinds of social organisation and, I would argue, world-views.

Wherever I have looked, I've found that the traditionally nomadic ways of life are under enormous pressure (there may be exceptions, but they only prove the rule), and will, I believe, soon disappear. Given that we have been nomadic since our time as *Homo sapiens sapiens* (the wisest of the wise) began – about 200,000 years ago – and given that we have lived in settlements for less than 10,000 of those years, that strikes me as an extraordinary fact.

During those 10,000 years we have made massive and irreversible changes to the environment, creating problems for ourselves that we may not be able to solve. It's as if we have come to believe that there is something inherent in our species that makes such destruction inevitable, that it has nothing to do with economic and political systems, but with humanness itself. But for 200,000 years, culture and nature got on just fine. Even if it were true that early humans knocked out the big game wherever they went (and school is still very much out on that score), one only need look at present-day hunter-gatherer societies to see that they learnt from their mistakes. Preservation of the environment on which they depend is encoded in their cosmologies.

In Australia, for example, before the first agriculturalist arrived, there had been at least 60,000 years of a continual and very successful relationship between culture and nature. Culture – the exchange of ideas and the creation of new ways of thinking and imagining – that thing we do so much better than any other animal – presides over the determinism of our DNA. And with luck, new ways of thinking and imagining will lead to reversing the destructive trend before it is too late.

New ideas arise out of reassessing older ones. What is useful in those discarded ideas? What is harmful in the ones we supplanted them with? Perhaps all retrospection is melancholy because it leads to an understanding of what we have lost. But without it we cannot make the future. We get out of cul-de-sacs by retracing our steps to find out where we went wrong.

This essay suggests that one wrong turning occurred when we gave up cultures of movement for cultures of accumulation. I do not mean to say that we should (or could) return to traditional nomadic economies. I do mean to say that there are systems of knowledge, and grand poetical schemata derived from the mobile life, that it would be foolish to disregard or underrate. And mad to destroy.

The French translation of "wandering" is l'errance, the Latin root of which means to make a mistake. By our errors we see deeper into life. We learn from them.

I offer this essay not as a solution to our ecological woes. I don't pretend to know the answers to the questions it raises. I offer it merely as a ground for reflection, a literary errance. ◊

Robyn Davidson

NO FIXED ADDRESS | Nomads and the Fate of the Planet

Robyn Davidson

INDIAN HIMALAYAS

The house sits at 7,000 feet. To the south-west, just visible through a gap in the hills which are like stacked slices of ever paler blue glass, is the Gangetic Plain, under a pall of dust. To the north-east, the rampart of rock and ice that is the Himalayas proper, on the other side of which lies Tibet. To reach the house from the nearest road, one must climb through 3,000 feet of Himalayan oak forest, along a rough path. One must hire ponies or men to carry all the luggage and provisions up to the house.

I love this place and would like to be buried here.

When I say "this place", of course I don't just mean the house and its setting. I mean the people who live around me, some of whom work for me as servants, gardeners, stonemasons, porters and so on. I provide one of the very few opportunities for employment in these hills.

Most of the original oak from this area – the Kumaon – was taken out by the British during the world wars. They replaced it with introduced pine which dries out the soil and inhibits the seeding of native species. The 400 acres on which I live is re-growth native oak, and one of the few patches of it in the Kumaon region. Every time I drive from the railhead to the village below, on my way back here from Australia or London, I notice another hillside thinned of timber, another patch of forest uprooted to make a tiny terraced field, another landslide on these geologically new, precipitous inclines.

The peasants are wholly aware that they are responsible for their forest disappearing, for their water disappearing, but they have no choice. If they do not chop wood, how will they cook and stay warm? If they do not carve out new fields from the forest, what will their sons do? As it is, many have to go to towns and cities to find work. If they do not have several children, who will take care of them when they are old, or provide the labour needed when the crops are ready? Many children die, after all. If they do not lop the trees for feed for their animals, or allow them to graze in the forest, the animals will starve. If they do not snare the leopards, or poison them, the leopards will take their animals or, worse still, their children. With the loss of forest goes the loss of game, and that makes for hungry leopards. There is no safety net for the peasants here. One stroke of bad luck, and total, irremediable ruin is their fate. Here, poverty is the cause of ecological catastrophe, not ignorance, not greed.

The farms are small, hand-made terraces radiating down cleared hillsides. Three or four crops are grown in a year – wheat, corn, potatoes, cabbage, peas. The work is backbreaking, the yield, subsistence. The weather is harsh – freezing winters, hail in spring, dry early summers, a late summer monsoon which washes soil down into the river far below. Ploughing is done with oxen. Monkeys, pigs, bears and deer take their portion of crop yields. With the clearing of oak, whose roots hold water in the catchment slopes, springs dry up. Domestic animals are taken out for grazing in the national forests and eat out any young oak, which is highly nutritious but slow-growing. Seedlings don't stand a chance against desiccation and over-grazing. Women range all day through the remaining forest, cutting wood for cooking fires, or gathering huge bundles of grass for their animals, which they carry home on their heads. They work unbelievably hard, but are in poor health due to poor nutrition. The diet is principally wheat flour, lentils, sugar, milk, a few vegetables and spice. Nevertheless they tend to have many pregnancies, despite the government's advertising campaign promoting two children only. That policy has nothing to do with the exigencies of their lives.

There are fights within families over land. Sons who cannot inherit have to find other farmland or work elsewhere. There is little arable land left, and that is prohibitively expensive. (A lot of it now is being bought up by developers, catering to the wealthy middle class who want to return to bucolic simplicity during their holidays, who build large cement houses containing all the mod cons, and clear any trees that spoil the view.) Dispossessed peasants must join the drain of rural people heading to the city. Usually they will live in poverty and squalor there, scraping enough to get by in menial jobs, or begging in the streets. Sometimes, if they have managed to sell land, they set up small businesses and join the burgeoning middle class on its bottom rung. Either way, life is precarious.

If there is a particularly bad year or two, so that the farms fall below subsistence, then most of the men will have to leave to find other work. Women must still go out almost all day to gather wood. Children are looked after by old people. Or they look after themselves. Children and old people must do all the farm labour. And that labour is great because it is a perpetual wrestling with the forest – keeping it back, digging it up, building fences against it, changing it, trying to stave off its fecund complexity for growth that is uniform and predictable. It's an all-day, all-night job, year in, year out, defying nature's processes. The peasants here are wary of change. It takes them a long time to try something new, to do things another way. They are not flexible people. There is no leeway for mistakes.

I am witnessing archaic agriculture at first hand – the aftershocks of the most important revolution the human race has ever undergone.

I have managed to keep my 400 acres of re-growth oak intact. No wood-cutting is allowed here; no farm animals graze in the forest. The women are invited to cut grass once a year, but they cannot lop and destroy the trees. At first they considered me an impediment to be got around. But when water began to flow back into their springs, the policy was accepted. Wildlife has begun to return to the area.

I like my neighbours very much. And I depend on them just as they depend on me. I would like to do something for them, apart from offering employment. I would like to set up a local industry in which they can participate. Tourism, for example. The stressed and alienated of the First World can come and enjoy the simplicity, sweetness and grace of the Third. If there is more money to be made in accommodating and serving such visitors than in farming, then the remaining forest can be preserved. And from a more secure economic base improvements in the peasants' quality of life can be generated. Those benefits of modern civilisation such as effective medicine and literacy. The easing of daily anxiety, of internecine squabbling and land grabbing, of grinding, bone-cracking labour. Everyone will benefit.

Well, perhaps not everyone. Not in the long term, anyway. Not in relation to the Big Picture.

My neighbours use incomparably less of the world's resources than tourists do. Than I do. I drive a car. I dash around the world in aeroplanes. I use washing machines and forget to turn off electric lights. I throw out more garbage in a week than these peasants would in a year.

As a product of the First World, I enjoy a better standard of living than ever before in history. But that is because I belong to an elite, dependent on materials imported from countries with large, impoverished populations. I live on a higher step of a pyramidal social structure that gradually formed around the settled life, and continues to be essential to the world economy. It is a myth that globalising, free-market capitalism will secure everyone a position at the top. We know perfectly well that the earth's resources simply could not cope – are already not coping. For some of us to retain the standard of living we have become used to, others of us will have to provide the cheap labour, and remain poor. I might be able to help a few peasants up onto a higher level of the pyramid, but their vacated rung will quickly be filled by others less fortunate.

The agricultural revolution led directly to the benefits people like me enjoy. But they are available to the few at the expense of the many. This is axiomatic.

> And Adam knew Eve his wife; and she conceived, and bare Cain, and said, I have gotten a man from the Lord.
> And she again bare his brother Abel. And Abel was a keeper of sheep, but Cain was a tiller of the ground.
> And in process of time it came to pass, that Cain brought of the fruit of the ground an offering unto the Lord.
> And Abel, he also brought of the firstlings of his flock and of the fat thereof. And the Lord had respect unto Abel and to his offering:
> But unto Cain and to his offering he had not respect. And Cain was very wroth, and his countenance fell.
> And the Lord said unto Cain, Why art thou wroth? and why is thy countenance fallen?
> If thou doest well, shalt thou not be accepted? and if thou doest not well, sin lieth at the door: and unto thee shall be his desire, and thou shalt rule over him.
> And Cain talked with Abel his brother: and it came to pass, when they were in the field, that Cain rose up against Abel his brother, and slew him.
> And the Lord said unto Cain, Where is Abel thy brother? And he said, I know not: Am I my brother's keeper? And he said, What hast thou done? the voice of thy brother's blood crieth unto me from the ground.
> And now art thou cursed from the earth, which hath opened her mouth to receive thy brother's blood from thy hand.

When thou tillest the ground, it shall not henceforth yield unto thee her strength; a fugitive and a vagabond shalt thou be in the earth.

And Cain said unto the Lord, My punishment *is* greater than I can bear.

Behold, thou hast driven me out this day from the face of the earth; and from thy face shall I be hid; and I shall be a fugitive and a vagabond in the earth; and it shall come to pass, that every one that findeth me shall slay me.

And the Lord said unto him, Therefore whosoever slayeth Cain, vengeance shall be taken on him sevenfold. And the Lord set a mark upon Cain, lest any finding him should kill him.

And Cain went out from the presence of the Lord, and dwelt in the land of Nod, on the east of Eden.

And Cain knew his wife; and she conceived, and bare Enoch: and he builded a city, and called the name of the city, after the name of his son, Enoch.

I read this Genesis allegory as a brief history of prehistory, the rise of agriculture and settlement, and, eventually, the creation of cities or, as we like to call it, civilisation.

Eden is the state of animality, before language and imagination set us apart from other animals. Man is "evicted" from this state, into the pain of self-consciousness and awareness of mortality.

At a point in the story, there is a divergence. Cain plants crops and remains in one place. Abel continues to wander, either as a hunter-gatherer or as a herdsman-hunter.

Cain's agricultural produce is inferior to Abel's. It is high-calorie, low-protein, homogeneous bulk. The starchy grain can feed more people but at a lower standard of nutrition. Cain's workers have much less leisure time than their nomadic cousins who are not only healthier, they are not afflicted by periodic famine. In hard times they can move elsewhere to find food.

Compared to Abel of the wilderness, Cain and his people are short, overworked and full of parasites. Their teeth are rotten. Their mortality rate is high. Their bones are rickety, and they suffer from the infectious diseases and epidemics that cannot exist among people who shift around all the time. Women of Cain have lost much of their autonomy. They have far more pregnancies than women of Abel, because farmers need lots of children as a labour force.

There are, therefore, many more Cains than Abels. And even though they are wormy and stunted and malnourished, their unprecedented numbers can defeat, or simply subsume, small bands of nomads.

Cain is no longer his "brother's keeper" in the sense that individual possession of stored food takes the place of the food-sharing habits of nomads. Hunter-gatherers don't produce surplus, and they can't carry much weight. Therefore there is virtually no social ranking or dominance of the kind needed to hoard, redistribute, steal or protect excess food. Abel's people are essentially egalitarian (as modern nomads still are). Men and women together contribute to the survival of the group, with women often providing the majority of calories.

Cain continues to plant crops on land that begins to lose its fertility. Or he's faced with a drought, or eroding flood, or the land is divided up among too many descendants so there's no longer enough of it for subsistence. Descendants who cannot inherit have to go elsewhere, as "vagabonds, fugitives", to find new land to cultivate. Wherever they go in country given over to agriculture, they are threatened and turned away. There is no room for them and they must resort to reclaiming land from the "jungle". There they must drive off, incorporate or kill competing nomads.

Self-sufficient villages form. The house becomes the centre of an entirely new social organisation and locus of production. Women's range of activity shrinks further. The new code of domestic morality is about the safeguarding of property, and that includes her. Her protection is also captivity. People have to find new ways to organise private and public space, new ways to describe time, new ways to socialise, new ways to cope with friction and with violence. Alcohol enters the scene. Cain is the first drunk.

Greater food surpluses lead to more complex settlements requiring specialists – full-time craftsmen, priests and chiefs. A nascent elite controls the resources of increasing numbers of people. Society, already stratified by the altered requirements of agriculture, begins to segregate and separate further, into classes and castes. Rulers grow in power, reinforcing their authority through warrior castes whose role is to accrue and protect wealth. Different professions acquire different ranks. Social opportunity declines as boundaries harden between groups.

Walls are now necessary, because surplus food stored behind them attracts raiders. There were war-like skirmishes in Abel's world too, of course. But now, for the first time, there is surplus worth stealing, making warfare chronic.

When these societies coalesce into cities, part two of the agricultural revolution begins. The urban revolution. It is characterised by high-density living, hierarchy, bureaucracy, regimentation and a ruling class in command of a farming underclass. The social pyramid necessary for intensified agricultural production to feed the city is locked into place, including the coercive institutions needed to hold it all together – armies, tax collectors, police, religious institutions. Warfare develops beyond raiding to conquest and subjugation. It is aggrandised into an "heroic" calling. In a habitat already filled, the losers cannot just go away and form a new community. There is now nowhere to go. Defeated groups are either killed or enslaved.

Abel's people are driven almost to extinction. The old habitats, once rich in game and wild foods, have been transformed and can no longer sustain them. All that is left to them is land that farmers cannot use – deserts, frozen tundra, high-altitude pastures. Everywhere else, the domestic has replaced the wild, and the change is irreversible.

The new economic mode is not without advantages. Specialised groups of artists and artisans can produce "great" architecture, and the "great" art adorning it. But it belongs to the Nobles and the Priests. The tallying necessary for bureaucrats measuring and trading grain evolves into writing, which stores cultural information. But it is only accessible to the educated elite. Goods, power and information thus condense at the top of the pyramid. In nomadic societies, the entire culture is encapsulated in each individual.

Cain's people have traded immersion in nature for domination of it. In order to eat, they have to keep nature at bay, hacking back jungle growth, uprooting weeds, changing water systems for irrigation, clearing forest for new fields. Nature becomes an opponent, something subservient to human will. They have changed from Homo *sapiens sapiens* to Homo *arrogans*.

Hobbes' vision of humanity's dystopia before the invention of the plough – "No arts; no letters; no society; and which is worst of all, continual fear and danger of violent death; and the life of man, solitary, poor, nasty, brutish, and short" – would better describe the life of a penniless ex-peasant, living away from his family in a city, than it would, say, that of a traditional Aborigine. The streets of Delhi and Bombay are filled with such souls:

> His poor self,
> A dedicated beggar to the air,
> With his disease of all-shunned poverty,
> Walks, like contempt, alone.
> —William Shakespeare, Timon of Athens

The Western Queensland cattle station where I was born was rather small by outback standards. It was dry country, just beyond the Darling Downs, but not the kind of desert that demands a few million acres to run a profit on livestock.

Our land was relatively untouched – had been minimally cleared, and never ploughed. Leichhardt passed across it on one of his expeditions inland, leaving an L-marked tree up in our brigalow forest. A dry white-sand river-bed, lined by eucalypts, snaked along a hundred metres from the house – a simple, weatherboard building on stilts, flanked by rainwater tanks that had been empty for years, and gauzed verandahs. A windmill clanked all day. There was a tin shed for storing hay and saddlery for the stock horses. My father ran Hereford cattle, and never overstocked. By the time I came along, he was wealthy enough to buy a ute. Before that the only transport was horse and cart.

He was a very knowledgeable naturalist and geologist, and he loved the bush with a passion. He'd walked around East Africa for many years, between the wars, alternately harpooning crocodiles and prospecting for gold. He was a man's man, Edwardian in spirit, empirical as an English-man, but a bit of a dreamer. He was happiest when he was alone out bush, boiling a billy and watching nature perform around him. There were many deadly snakes in that area, but they didn't worry him at all. If they were in or near the house, he'd catch them behind the head, let them coil around his arm, then take them down to the river-bed and let them go. He taught me basic astronomy and geology before I was six, and it was from him I absorbed my love of the natural world, and con-fidence within it.

He was from a long line of Queensland squattocracy – grazier pioneers whose legacy was a sense of upper-class entitlement. They were marked by eccentricity and haughtiness, a dislike of the pettiness and restrictions of the middle class, yet a direct and usually affectionate relationship with their workers. They talked about the blacks as being "bush aristocrats" or "poor old Abos". When Aborigines were taken off the stations to be sent to Mission Reserves, my forebears were dead against it, believing the blacks would be better off staying on their country. There are photographs of "the blacks' camp", women dressed in long skirts and high-necked Victorian blouses, men in stockman's gear, humpies made of mulga and tin.

Even as a child (and all the indigenous people had long gone by then), I felt that Stanley Park was missing something. And whatever that something was, gave the land a mournful quality. All that blinding, drenching light, yet you got the sense there was darkness in it. Like the backing on a mirror.

The only information I had about "poor old Abos" was from my father saying how sad it was that they had to die out. Survival of the fittest made this inevitable. I pored over a book called *Customs of the World*, published in the '20s, which showed photographs of naked men wearing tall head-dresses of feathers and paint. I held in my hand the stone axes, spears and the pointing bone that my father had collected, or been given, and thought about the other hands that had held them, during those incomprehensibly long reaches of previous time.

My father loved natural bushland, but this did not prevent him from "improving" it. He would go out on his horse before dawn, up to the escarpment brigalow, to ringbark those tough little trees with his axe. No doubt he could see, even then, that once the brigalow was gone, erosion followed quickly enough in that barren white soil. But the impenetrable brigalow made mustering difficult, so it had to go.

My father sold up after a seven-year drought had drained his bank account dry. The drought was broken by a fantastic storm, and I remember a foot of hail around the house – my first encounter with ice. Then the river came down – swirling mud-coloured torrents carrying torn-up trees, breaking its banks and threatening to take our house with it. There was no capital left with which to shore up the river-bank against the next floods. So we sold Stanley Park to a gentleman farmer with pots of money, and moved east.

In all the time that whitefellas had lived among blackfellas, it had not occurred to the former that they might have a great deal to learn from the latter. That was a thought it was impossible to have, because Aborigines were the children of the race of man, and you don't take children's reasoning seriously.

Such are the forms of delusion that can occur when systems of belief obscure the obvious.

Christian missionaries and government worked together to save the souls of the blacks, and the first step towards conversion was to instil a Protestant, agriculture-based work ethic. Flierl, a Lutheran missionary in North Queensland, stated, for example, that "the Aboriginals are nomads. Nothing can be done among them without settling them down on reserves. They are not used to hard work, and very slow in leaving their former manners and customs …"

His successor Pfalzer extended that view with: "The only thing that could keep these widely roaming hordes together at all is work. But if they are to work they must be fed. And we will not have the necessary food for them unless we cultivate the land."

Ritual maintenance of sacred sites was prevented, sundering people from their country, which is to say, from meaning and identity. Trauma after trauma was inflicted, sometimes viciously, sometimes with indifference, and sometimes with good intentions.

So it must have been, in some form or another, along the interface between settlement and nomadism, for 10,000 years.

The ideology ingrained in my father was Social Darwinism. It allowed him to believe that it was regrettable, even tragic, but ultimately unavoidable that a race and all its achievements should disappear, that the people who had worked for your family and helped them build up their cattle stations could be evicted from their own land and shunted off somewhere, never to be seen again. The words "concentration camp" had not entered the vernacular, and Robespierre's dictum that you had to break eggs to make omelettes had not yet been ironised. Faith in limitless progress fostered the belief that the beloved bush could be carved up into small parcels, emptied of wildlife that competed with stock, radically transformed and turned to the production of wealth, without any unpleasant kickback.

When I think back to Stanley Park now, I see it as a palimpsest of two modes of thinking. There was nomadic thinking: nomads range over country, allowing foraged areas to recuperate. Their survival is secured principally through observing and working with their environment, rather than battling against it. Then there was the kind of thinking that arose when humans became sedentary and began to conceive of land as something that could be possessed, dominated, transformed. It was the beginning of a detached perspective: its emblem, the fence.

In Aboriginal society a boundary or border is not a fixed line of division so much as a fuzzy set of relationships – interchanges of rights and duties, like pathways – across shared territory. Flexibly bounded places, or Countries, might be occupied by different cultural groups, speaking different languages, and sometimes antagonistic to each other, but nevertheless linked at a higher conceptual level by the net-like structure of the Dreaming – the original "theory of everything".

Scholars are still trying to describe the "Dreaming" in such a way as to make it accessible to non-Aboriginal understanding. Firstly, the word itself is something of a linguistic cock-up by an anthropologist attempting to translate an Arrernte word "Altyerre" – the meaning of which is largely unrelated to the English notion of dreams. T.G.H. Strehlow thought that a better translation would be "Eternal, Uncreated".

Difficulties arise not just because of the immense complexity of traditional Aboriginal world-views (which are also changing in response to immigrant ideas), but because of differences in the very foundations of descriptions of reality. We all believe our world constructs must be universal. The Western mind assumes that a linear time progression – marked off along its infinite stretch by remote, recent, present, soon, far-off – is the natural, even innate, orientation. It is difficult to imagine a consciousness in which that way of thinking is all but absent, in which history is absorbed into changelessness, and events (temporality) are turned into places.

No matter how much I read about the Dreaming, the confidence that I understand it never quite takes root in my mind. To me it is on a par with, say, quantum mechanics, or string theory – ideas you think you grasp until you have to explain them. Each time I attempt it, I have to feel my way into it again, and I am never sure of my ground.

One could say that the Dreaming is a spiritual realm which saturates the visible world with meaning; that it is the matrix of being; that it was the time of creation; that it is a parallel universe which may be contacted via the ritual performance of song, dance and painting; that it is a network of stories of mythological heroes – the forerunners and creators of contemporary man.

During the creation period, the ancestral beings made journeys and performed deeds: they fought, loved, hunted, behaved badly or well, rather like the Greek gods, and where they camped or hurled spears or gave birth, tell-tale marks were left in the earth. While creating this topography, they were morphing constantly from animal to human and back to animal, again rather like the Greeks.

They made separate countries, but interlaced them (related them) with their story tracks. They created frameworks for kin relations. Many different ancestors created a country, by travelling across it and meeting each other. In that way, a particular country is shared by all the creatures who live there, their essences arising from the Dreaming, and returning to it. Some Dreamings crossed many countries, interacting with local ones as they went, and connecting places far from each other. Thus the pulse of life spreads, blood-like, through the body of the continent – node/pathway, node/pathway – as far as, and sometimes into, the sea.

At the end of that epoch, exhausted by their work, they sank back into the ground at sacred sites, where their power remains in a condensed form.

It's not quite right, however, to say that the creation period is in the past, because it is a past that is eternal and therefore also present. Ancestors sink back into, but also emerge from and pass through, sites. In other words, an ancestor's journey, or story, became a place, and that place holds past, present and future simultaneously.

For traditionally oriented Aboriginal people, the historical past lies a couple of generations back, *and it always will*. The Dreaming encompasses and surrounds this time of living memory, which sinks into it. Time sinks into place, into Country.

Each sacred site contains a potentially limitless supply of the particular species left there by an ancestor. But in order to ensure their continued generation, ceremonial action is required. If this isn't done, or isn't done properly, that life-form will eventually disappear. Children, too, are born from the ancestor's spirit which arises out of its place to impregnate a woman. Such children belong to and have responsibility for that place, and will return to it after death, so that its life potential isn't dissipated.

Not only did the mythical ancestors give the world its shape, they imbued it with moral and social structures – handing down laws whereby all humans have equal intrinsic value and a share of goods. Living by these laws invigorates the life-force surging and burgeoning through the land. In fact, to sing a ritual song is to move that ancestor along through the land. Earth is sacred, sentient stuff; it is not a counterpoint to heaven. Heaven and earth are embedded together, on the same plane. A country is saturated in consciousness. It recognises and responds to people. It *depends* on people. And just as people torn from their country are lost in non-meaning, country without its people is "orphaned" and in peril. When the web of the Dreaming is torn, the consequences for land and life are dire.

In other words, there is no distinction between the material and the spiritual, so ancestor, story, place, painting, ritual object, song and singer are all, in essence, the same thing. Dreaming tracks (or stories or songs) lace the whole of the continent. Australia itself is a narrative.

It's as if the creative potential of a whole culture, instead of being dissipated on the production of material wealth, has concentrated itself into the never-ending translation of all phenomena into one elegant, all-encompassing symbol. It is this astonishing intellectual feat that allowed indigenous people to inhabit this country so successfully, and for so long. Not just a knowledge of the landscape as a surface of separate things, but an engagement with the deeper processes and patterns and connections between things. Patterns, connections, pathways: these are emphasised. Agricultural world-views shift that emphasis to abstract geometry, division and separation, boundaries.

Traditionally oriented Aborigines are constantly on the move but paradoxically they are existentially the most stationary people on earth. Like the Dreamings, they move eternally along the tracks and networks, but remain rooted in and identified with certain places. The ancestors stopped travelling and sank into sacred sites, but they are also simultaneously present at each of the many sites along their creation journey. They are eternally travelling and eternally fixed, like the human beings who created them and were created by them. People of the Dreaming are always "at home" in the deepest possible sense.

Compare that to extreme forms of the detached perspective that agriculture gave us. The Rapture fundamentalists, for example, who ecstatically await the end of the world which, they say, should be any day now. Things like global warming, wars in the Middle East, and ecological collapse are signs of the prophesied apocalypse, and they are to be encouraged because after Armageddon, Christ will take up true believers, of which there are frighteningly large numbers – several million it is said. For them heaven is our true home; earth, expendable rubbish.

It is a pathology that places man so far outside nature, so alienated from the earth, that he would happily destroy it entirely. In its place, pyramid heaven, with a life-hating God on top.

I don't pretend to have entered the consciousness of a traditional Aboriginal person. But I imagine sometimes what it might feel like to have such a different perspective. Is it a nowness that spreads out into the place you are in, containing the flow of time? Rather like that trance-like state we experienced as children when everything seemed to unfold in an enormous billowing present. Or perhaps it is like a piece of music – a unity which nevertheless unfolds heterogeneously through time. It is said that when Mozart opened a musical manuscript he hadn't seen before, he "heard" the piece all at once, all in the same moment.

Aboriginal culture was always responding to change, always dynamic. But after colonisation, it had to make sense of the tidal wave of otherness overwhelming it. The Dreaming is changing rapidly in response to those challenges, but it continues to try to mend itself, in order to keep life going.

But I knew nothing about it then. And it would be twenty years before I met an indigenous Australian.

TIBET

The flight from Kathmandu to Lhasa, past Everest and its cousins, must be the most spectacular in the world. Carved into the landscape beneath, the geological past is as easy to read as a book: two continents crash into each other, waves of percussion take form in rock, the bed of a sea is squeezed up until it becomes the planet's highest plateau on which little puddles of sea remain in the form of vast and salty lakes. It is from this "roof" that most of Asia's great rivers tumble, including the Yangtse and the Yellow.

From here the steppes and deserts of Central and Inner Asia stretch north to the mountains of Mongolia and beyond to the Siberian taiga, forming the largest natural pastureland in the world. Its grasses clothe most of the Tibet Autonomous Region (TAR) and four other Chinese provinces – the "Western regions" where China's ethnic minorities are concentrated.

Past the glass-sharp peaks, the "hills" of the plateau look like tawny velvet thrown over bones. Some are dusted with summer snow. The Yarlung Tsangpo River (Brahmaputra), must be at least two miles wide, swollen by seasonal rains, its opacity representing millions of tons of mountain, worn and torn down by water. Along valleys, there are tiny pockets of arable land containing the only grain that will thrive at this altitude – barley. There are minute, walled plantations of willow and poplar on the banks of the river. Higher than that, not a tree to be seen. That arduous, wind-battled niche belongs to nomadic herders. I have come to witness for myself one of the last great examples of a way of life once common in many regions of the world. From what I have read, Tibetan pastoralists have escaped the bleak future facing nomads in other countries, because at this altitude, and in this astonishingly unpredictable and ferocious weather, they have no competitors.

The origin of pastoralism has been much debated. Some scholars, assuming the superiority of settled cultures over nomadic, believed it to be an evolutionary stage in human progress, wedged between hunting-gathering and agriculture. But recent archaeological data suggest that agriculture actually preceded it. Perhaps proto-farmers selectively bred wild animals, and when their herds grew too large to graze locally, some took to nomadic pastoralism. Or perhaps early nomads managed wild animals, much as reindeer-herding Sami still do in regions of the sub-Arctic. Probably different forms developed frequently and spasmodically across different environments, with different domesticable species. But no one knows for sure. Nomads don't leave much material evidence behind them.

Livestock provide fresh food on the hoof: that is, it keeps from spoiling until needed. Secondary products – milk, yogurt, cheese, fertiliser and fuel – can be bartered with farmers, a trade that must have lubricated the interface between settlement and nomadism, leading to a somewhat symbiotic relationship, but with ancient suspicions built in. Nomads outside city walls can always turn to raiding. And from the other perspective, small bands of herders are usually no match for punitive armies.

However you imagine its origins, pastoral nomadism put to use the intimate knowledge hunters had of animals. Herders continued to rely on those first principles that humans had developed throughout their history – observing, learning from and accommodating themselves to the natural world. Ultimately, pastoral nomadism provided an alternative to the sedentary cultures of agricultural and urban societies.

Here on the Tibetan Plateau, it was made possible by the domestication of wild yak. Later, horses, sheep and goats were included, making for complicated mixed herding methods, with different animals requiring different pasture, and grazing at different bands of altitude.

Effective management requires constantly moving the herds to the best pasture possible during the short summer growing season. The animals must lay down enough fat in those few months to survive the plateau's appalling winter and a grim starvation spring. To accomplish that, a herder requires tremendous skill and knowledge.

Before the Chinese takeover, nomads were ruled by Buddhist lamas, in a quasi-feudal estate system. They owned their own herds, and whatever products they didn't consume themselves were bartered for barley and tea. Family members jointly managed their animals, without interference from the lamas, who, in return for tax revenue, mediated disputes and provided religious services. The nomads couldn't graze their herds wherever they chose, but individuals could travel freely and pilgrimage was an important part of social and spiritual life. There was class mobility too – anyone could enter the nobility through government or military service, and anyone could embark on a religious career. Sometimes pastoral nomads increased income by trading – travelling to Ladakh, Nepal, India, China and Mongolia. Tibetan society was a mediaeval mélange of nomads, traders, farmers, hunters, bandits, merchants, monks, nuns, pilgrims and artists, united in the main by Bon-influenced Buddhism.

Modernity arrived in October 1950, when the communist Chinese Army marched into Eastern Tibet. The occupation was initially orderly, but chaos followed soon enough, ultimately resulting in over a million Tibetan deaths, the destruction of thousands of monasteries and temples, and the flight of the Dalai Lama to Dharamsala in India, where the Government in Exile now resides. Hollywood popularity and audiences with Bill Clinton notwithstanding, the chances of a "free Tibet" are vanishingly slim, and the Tibetans remaining in their "land of snows" make accommodation with the new dispensation as best they can. There is no doubt that some are materially better off than ever before. The problem is that those most benefiting are necessarily the most deracinated. The values of Chinese communism (atheism, materialism) do not mix well with the values of Buddhism. And a unique interpretation of Buddhism is at the very heart of Tibetan civilisation and identity.

It was during the Cultural Revolution, from 1966 to the '80s, that the nomads (like everyone else in China) suffered the most. Religion, so central to their identity, was banned, practitioners persecuted, and the private ownership of livestock was replaced by people's communes. All the traditional grazing structures were dismantled, and for the first time the grasslands felt the bite of the plough. That era was an ecological, social and moral catastrophe.

It ended with the ousting of the Gang of Four. Then under Deng Xiaoping's leadership, modernisation replaced class struggle as China's dominant propaganda. The communes were dismantled; livestock was returned to family ownership. Since then, meat has become popular with China's burgeoning middle class, cashmere wool is selling well on the international market, and the expanding towns of new Tibet provide local markets for livestock products.

Pastoralism has recuperated to such an extent that the nomads of the Tibetan region are doing pretty well.

That, as I say, is what I have read.

The Chinese-built road from the airport is impressive. Where once pilgrims limped into the capital after many trials of will, I am swept towards my goal at a swift post-industrial clip, in a brand-new Land-Cruiser. A centuries-old nunnery flashes by the left window; a cliff where Guru Rinpoche impaled a daemon zips past the right. The road is a strip of modernity through previous time.

Lhasa is no Shangri-la, certainly, but there are wide streets, VW taxis assembled in Beijing, gimcrack apartment blocks – all the crassness and glitter of an opportunistic materialism let loose on the frontier, but no worse, and in some ways better, than many developing Asian towns. It is clear what the employment opportunities will be. Tourism, construction, small businesses, government jobs from which to pocket a retirement fund of corruption money, and crime. It is also immediately apparent that most of the jobs are taken by immigrant Han Chinese, fallouts of China's new economic policies, who have come to the borderlands for certain perquisites available there. They will work hard, save their cash, and return to their provinces as soon as they can. In Lhasa they outnumber Tibetans by two to one, and there is no love lost between the communities.

My plan is to attend a horse festival on the Chang Tang Plateau, a couple of hundred miles north of, and a thousand or so metres higher than, Lhasa. I'll take as many days as I like getting there, camping with different nomad families along the way, or spending night-halts in nunneries.

The jeep is booked and so are my driver, A-den, an ex-nomad, and my translator, Tenzing. We head out before dawn the next day.

Sunrise clips the tops of hills, and the clouds are just as Tibetan embroidery artists depict them – curly, with a tail. The light is blinding, even at this hour, and the shadows as sharp as blades. It is so hot along the road that we keep the windows open wide, but to our right, just a hundred yards away, a snow flurry whitens the slopes.

We stop at a little "restaurant" – a tiny room, grimy and gloomy, low tables and chairs, flasks of Tibetan butter tea, and a big television set showing DVD Chinese soaps. The street is churned-up mud. The weather has turned bleak and bitter, with tattered snow clouds driven along the sky. We are enjoying the balmy delights of high summer – that window of weather opportunity in which grasses and herbage can grow. Nomads are playing pool on tables set out in the street. Their physical beauty is matched by their sense of style – cowboy hats over plaits, full-length black coats, boots and white shirts. Others, their plaits tied up in red silk tassels, squat nearby selling chunks of yak that they cut from a carcass. We buy very good sirloin. (Yak meat, tsampa (barley flour) and buttery tea are what we will live on from now on.) All the little towns are more or less the same. The ubiquitous pool tables are there in the muddy streets, surrounded by handsome nomads. Some have a wild alcoholic look in their eyes. Eventually I ask why they aren't out with their herds, or working.

At first my companions are careful what they say. Everyone assumes that everyone else is spying for the Chinese, and it's often true. But soon enough they are setting me straight regarding what I have read – a process of re-education that will continue throughout this preliminary foray, and later, when I meet researchers in the field.

Unprecedented sandstorms erupted from China's Western regions recently and threatened to stifle Beijing. There was unprecedented flooding of the Yangtse. And unprecedented drought. And disappearing lakes. Consequently, the government is investing vast sums of money in environmental projects in those regions, one aspect of which is to "improve livestock production". International development agencies and the World Bank provide the ideology for these projects, which look convincing on paper because they use eco-speak to claim that traditional ways of using grasslands are detrimental to both profit and habitat. In other words, the nomads are responsible for the ecological destruction now causing such anxiety to the Chinese state.

The solution is to transform them into sedentary cattle farmers, such as we have here in Australia. To quote a government document, this will involve "changing the traditional and backward ideas of the pastoralists, and constructing a new pastoral region with the co-ordinated development of material civilisation, spiritual civilisation and ecological civilisation ..." In other words, agri-science, settlement and free enterprise.

The steppe, symbolic of a kind of wild, marauding freedom, which in all time has not been marked by a physical fence, is to be parcelled up into stock enclosures and paddocks, and planted with improved (introduced) grasses.

And all nomads are to be housed.

Unsurprisingly, the nomads themselves have not been consulted for this next great leap forward, despite an expertise gathered over generations, which has allowed them to make a living in surely the most difficult landscape on earth. Such knowledge is regarded as a hindrance to progress.

It is something of an *idée fixe* that nomads in marginal environments "overgraze" and therefore damage their pastures. Because they keep their stock numbers as high as possible at all times, it is assumed that grasses never fully regenerate. But contemporary research shows that high stock rates don't destroy pasture, *as long as herds remain mobile.* Nevertheless, the unsubstantiated assumption keeps re-circulating until it becomes received wisdom.

Tibetan nomads argue that the weather is so harsh, so unpredictable that even the best pastoralist can lose an entire herd in a winter storm, or a drought, or through some other random calamity. Increasing herd size during good years provides necessary insurance against such inevitable misfortunes. The strategy also makes for genetically strong animals; weak ones simply don't make it. Proof of the pudding is that this system has worked for millennia without damaging the pastures.

But when herds are kept in one place, nodes of over-grazing are inevitable. As the case studies coming out of Central Asia indicate, it is decreased access to traditional migration routes and increased no-go areas that cause soil compaction and advancing desertification.

Mobility is essential not just to the success of herding, but to social life as well. When animals are fenced in, the shepherds have little work to do. Women still have to keep a household functioning, still have to milk the animals, make cheese, and so on. But men with time on their hands gravitate to the towns to drink and play pool.

The new policy builds houses for the nomads and offers monetary incentives to abandon pastoralism. But the houses are often in newly constructed towns, completely off the rangelands. There are no jobs in these towns. Where there are jobs, in cultivation for example, these are usually contracted out to Han Chinese farmers from the east, or to locals who are better qualified.

When I asked A-den whether nomads could set up their own enterprises, he said: "To start up a business, you need good connections and money, and we who have lived as herders on the Chang Tang – where would we find either? I myself am illiterate. I have left the herds because I do not wish my children to suffer as I have. They must have an education. They must learn Chinese, and find good jobs. I am very lucky to have this job as a driver. It is because I can speak a little Chinese."

Wherever we drive that first day, modernity is constantly present in the form of a massive railway construction, connecting Lhasa with China. "You have to admit," I say, "that is an extraordinary engineering feat. And isn't it good that Tibetans can travel cheaply into China?"

Tenzing gives me a look and replies, "It will mean cheap travel for Chinese immigrants coming to take Tibetan jobs. And a cheap way for China to empty Tibet of its minerals."

We had intended to spend the first night in a monastery, but the road up to it is an impassable bog. A-den prevails upon a "rich" nomad lady to let us stay in her house. She is a fabulous-looking woman, carrying herself with confidence and poise. She is alone in the house, while her men are away shepherding in the summer pastures. Her fourteen-year-old daughter is herding female yaks, alone, up in the higher meadows.

The mother holds no concern for the girl at all. She takes for granted her ability and knowledge. They will be reunited in a couple of days.

The woman and her family would fit the statistic of "settled" nomads, but this is something of an illusion. The truth is that many "sedentary" families are still nomadic, only returning in winter to their houses. And even those who have settled permanently, and no longer own animals, refer to themselves, and indeed think of themselves, as nomads.

So far I've experienced no altitude problems, other than sudden attacks of narcolepsy. Like everyone else, I have had to shit outside, in the rain and hail. I am cold, wet, and I long for sleep. The rain pours down. Thunder roars and rattles around the mountains, lightning illuminates the monastery up above, stuck to its crag like a barnacle. The lady notices that I am in danger of falling face down into my boiled yak meat. She wraps me in a blanket, leads me to my cot and stokes the kitchen fire. I drift off while they murmur on, firelight flickering on her kitchen walls where large paper portraits of Deng and local communist officials gaze benevolently down upon us.

In the morning, she quietly enquires if I have a photo of the Dalai Lama with me and, if so, might she have it. Possessing such a photo can land you in jail.

Over the following days, I meet or camp with many families – some rich, some poor – but all of them proud of what they do. Whenever I comment on how tough their lives are, they laugh and assure me that it isn't so. Compared to farmers, their lives are easy. Nomads never have to dig, or carry heavy weights, or plant crops. Nomads let nature do the work. Farmers on the other hand have to struggle day in, day out. They never have a moment to relax. The nomads see their environment as generous and benevolent. Which isn't to say that they aren't interested in improving their living conditions with such modern innovations as mobile phones and motorcycles.

There is a surprising variety of responses to fencing. Some say they want it; others say it leads to all kinds of problems and conflict. I begin to sense that they see the parcelling out of land as inevitable, and they want to grab something while the going is good. Who knows what the government will do next? If you wait, or stick to the old ways, you might miss out on everything. Nomads are nothing if not opportunistic.

In any case, fences seem to be a *fait accompli*. They mark the end of Tibet's open space, and the transformation of a unique way of life.

The desire to control nomads politically and to incorporate them into non-nomadic cultures must have existed since the beginning of cities, when that schism between the settled and the mobile occurred. The city or state became the centre; beyond it was the outsider, the marauder, the barbarian. The colonial assumption that the "other" must be raised from dark bestiality into the light of civilisation began right there.

Han Chinese ethnocentrism – the belief that the more Chinese you are, the more civilised; and conversely, the further from Beijing you are, the more barbaric – is 2,000 years old. Communism didn't alter it much. According to that view the borderlands can be elevated by being incorporated into the body of the Motherland. It is this gradual Sinicisation that many in those borderlands fear.

One day, we pass through a small, ugly town in order to visit A-den's daughter. She is attending a college there, and learning to speak Chinese. Another of these gloomy, treeless towns on the outskirts of which is a cement barracks. She lives there, in a one-room cell. It contains a television set which is showing the usual Chinese soaps. I think to myself that there could be nothing more symbolic of the sedentary life than a cement room containing a television set and a sofa. Nevertheless, she is dressed as a nomad. And, like her father, she thinks of herself as a nomad. They can never go back to their life on the range. But the colonisers will have to work very hard indeed to assimilate such people.

Nomadism is the best strategy to employ in fragile and marginal eco-systems: it is a resilient, rational response to a variety of unpredictable circumstances. Yet governments the world over seem intent on destroying it. States have always felt uneasy about peripatetic peoples, who have little respect for borders, are difficult to control, evade taxes and tend towards independence of spirit. They are almost universally seen as unproductive members of society. But perhaps their greatest crime, in our times, is that they do not participate fully in the conspicuous consumption of unneces-sary stuff. As a Mongolian proverb puts it:

> Supreme treasure – knowledge
> Middle treasure – children
> Lowest treasure – material wealth

Towards the end of our time together, A-den, Tenzing and I make a visit to a high-altitude lake – one of those puddles of primordial sea left behind when two tectonic plates collided. We drive up to yet another pass and as we climb, the rain turns to sleet which turns to needles of horizontal snow. The road is a rutted track beside a partly frozen stream. How do people survive here in winter? What are they made of?

At the top of the pass a howling wind claws at millions of prayer flags distributing compassionate verses throughout the universe. Ten minutes later we are descending beneath the clouds into a different world.

White peaks inscribe an horizon of pure blue. Below us, the lake, tur-quoise, extends beyond the reach of sight. Green pasturelands, flecked with sheep and goats, stretch from the lake shore to the hills, and above that are the darker dots of grazing yak. Yak-wool tents are distributed throughout the flocks, like black spiders ready to pounce on the white specks around them.

Some cloud appears out of nowhere, scudding low and fast, dying the water petrol-green. A sudden squall. Tiny hail peppers our heads.

We make a dash for one of the tents, past the blue truck parked outside it, past the lines of milking goats, past the shepherd's motorbike.

The heavy tent flap is lifted and we are welcomed inside. A dung fire is crackling away, sending shafts of smoke up through a gap in the black wool roof. There are pieces of furniture and carpets. Warmth, comfort and courtesy. A shrine, photographs, devotional objects and butter lamps. The lady of the house is making cheese on a portagas stove. She plunges her red hands into almost boiling milk, again and again, until long scoops of gluey substance form, which are hung out to dry like stockings on a clothesline. It is delicious – a tough mozzarella. I am given a bed to stretch out on, and a prickly rug which smells of lanoline. Everyone gathers around to drink the inevitable butter tea, and talk and laugh. I ask if there might be a horse I could hire, in order to visit the lama living in a cave on the far shores of the lake.

A couple of days later, I am invited into his well-appointed cave, equipped with portagas, Tibetan furniture, library and hundreds of butter lamps, to which he constantly attends. A woman – his wife? – lives in the cave next door, and brings tea.

Afterwards I head "home" across the grasslands, following the shores of the lake, on a willing little pony who gallops at the touch of a heel. There are no fences from horizon to horizon.

RAJASTHAN

When I first visited India, in 1978, the Australian desert was still very much with me. Only a year had passed since I emerged from it. Nine months of intense solitude, walking from the centre to the west coast, a distance of almost 2,000 miles. It was a journey that was to transform my life in ways I could never have predicted and from which, I think, I have never entirely returned.

I had arrived in Alice Springs with nothing but a peculiar idea and the stubbornness of youth. I would get myself some wild camels from the bush, train them to carry my gear, then wander around the desert with them. I wanted to *walk* my country, experience it at the pace which existed before mechanical speed violated our perception of time's relation to space. Most of all, I wanted to learn something about Aboriginal people. I had never seen an Aborigine. They were as remote from me as the ancient Greeks.

In 1977, after two years of preparation, I set out for the Indian Ocean. All those miles empty of footprints, unburdened by history's mistakes. I had learnt how to see that landscape as a garden – man's home before the plough.

Consequently the crowds of the Subcontinent on that first visit seemed unnatural and frightening to me. There was not a particle of India that had not serviced agricultural man – ploughed, thrown as pots, eaten, shat out, lifted as dust, ploughed again. The impulse to move freely was every-where restricted. Dogs and fences, forts and defensive walls, zenanas and spiked gates. The whole geography shaped by the safeguarding of prop-erty. Had I been capable of looking closer then, I might have asked myself why every kind of previousness miraculously survived there, including hunters and gatherers. The wonder of India: to absorb and let be. But I was too overwhelmed by the obvious to notice the subtle.

I spent a few weeks in Rajasthan, and chanced upon a caste of pastoral nomads – the Raika, or Rabari. It was thought they had entered India from the north about a thousand years before, and brought the camel with them. Since then they had spread throughout six northern states, and diversified their stock to include cattle, sheep and goats. The only reference I could find to them was in a nineteenth-century census report, in which they were described as camel thieves, cactus-eaters and stealers of wheat.

I was, even then, preoccupied with the idea of mobility and its effect upon culture. People who move around can't carry many goods. That fact alone shapes social forms in which some human qualities are encouraged while others are discouraged. The slowly gleaned insights concerning Aboriginal philosophy had made a deep impression on me. That culture had solved all the big problems using poetic or imaginative resources rather than material ones. Aboriginal people were at one end of the mobility spectrum, their society strictly egalitarian, hoarding nothing, its only hierarchy based on accumulated knowledge to which all members could aspire. They understood their environment as a humanised realm soaked with consciousness, which if hurt, or neglected, would unbalance life-forces and lead to chaotic disturbance. In the deepest possible sense, they were at home in the world, though paradoxically their "home" was a fluid, extended one. A home of pathways.

Were there similarities between those kinds of nomads, and these? Did mobility lead to certain characteristics held in common across the nomadic spectrum? In short, was nomadic thinking an antidote to the worst of human neuroses? Or was I indulging in romantic stereotype?

I returned, years later, with the intention of joining the Raika on yearly migration.

I thought it might take six months to find a representative family willing to take me with them. Almost a year passed in maddening frustration. Many groups were no longer migrating at all; some were only doing local circuits with diminished herds, and leaving the women at home. Those who were doing the big loop came up with every reason under the sun

why they wanted to, but could not, take me. They feared I would be kid-
napped for ransom, or that I wouldn't be able to keep up, or that I would
get ill and die. One particularly deflating excuse was that, as I was obviously a man dressed in women's clothes, I might make the women preg-
nant, which they would find difficult to explain to their husbands.

At the base of it all was the fear that if something happened to me, they
would be blamed. There were no safety nets for them, and migration had
become a dangerous business.

Previously farmers and pastoralists had enjoyed a somewhat symbiotic
relationship, the graziers providing the farmers with animal dung for their
fields. There was equilibrium between them, and enough open grazing
land to accommodate visiting as well as local animals. The relationship
between sedentary and peripatetic people had no doubt always required
diplomacy, but in recent times it had become potentially explosive.

The old patterns of migration, which on a map might look like ancient
river systems, were now more like feeble streams insinuating themselves
around countless obstructions, their changing beds containing local eddies
formed by a back-pressure of population. There was 50 per cent less land
available for grazing than just ten years before. Enormous increases in government wells had meant that newly irrigated farms clogged the migration
routes, turning natural pastureland into salty wastes after only a few years.
Small-scale peasants were usually close to destitution, so although they still
wanted the animals' dung, they did not want the incoming herds eating
their only crop or the local grasses that sustained their own stock. During
migration, fights were prevalent, people were killed, and when there was
trouble the police always took the side of sedentary folk, from whom they
skimmed off the bulk of their baksheesh. Pastoral areas sometimes spanned
not just internal borders but national ones. The Raika's mobility meant
they were treated as suspicious foreigners wherever they went. And governments never like nomads.

Droughts, military no-go areas, atomic testing sites, political boundaries, increasing population, closure of government forests, the spread of

subsidised agriculture, the claiming of land for industry, all these factors had forced the nomads to shift further and further south, out of the deserts and into greener parts of the country. Or they had forced them to settle.

In desperation I crossed into the neighbouring state of Gujarat, and almost immediately found what I was looking for. A village of Rabari about to set out with 5,000 sheep, twenty camels and fifty people, across the Little Rann of Kutch, into Saurashtra. Phagu, the mukki (leader of migration), conferred with his wife, Nakki, and with other members of the dang (migration). They gathered around me, throwing hand-made mats down for me to sit on, offering tea and excitedly asking questions. I knew my measure was being taken. Eventually Phagu announced that they would be happy to take me along. He would adopt me as his daughter, meaning I would be as much under his protection as his blood family.

I was to wedge my camp each night between two branches of my family. On one side, Phagu, Nakki, two grown-up daughters, a younger son and an eight-year-old daughter. On the other side, Phagu's brother, brother's wife and their daughter. Although I was closer to Nakki in age, it was really the three younger women who were my peers and with whom I was to spend most of my time. Jaivi was in her twenties, had the same dry humour as her father, and a face round and open as a sunflower. Parma, my "cousin", was tough and uncompromising, her beauty more masculine and ambiguous than Jaivi's. Latchi, Phagu's fifteen-year-old, regarded the world with that bored air that is so tiresome in adolescents and spent most of her time looking into her mirror. All were gruff in manner – a friendly pat was a thump; a playful touch, a whack. But then, at other moments, they would display the utmost delicacy in kissing a palm or touching a face. They were extraordinarily beautiful, but it wasn't just the black wool and silver they wore, or the kajal carefully applied to the eyes each morning, it was their poise. They carried themselves with the regal self-assurance of people who know their value, as free of deference as the wind.

These women owned property in their own right (receiving sheep from their husband's family at marriage and inheriting their mother's jewellery), and although they did not sit in panchayats, no one doubted who made the decisions back home. They were not burdened with child-bearing during their teens (and seldom had more than four children). Their work was as valued as the men's. They could shop and do business in villages and towns without being chaperoned and without covering their faces. I do not mean to say that individual women were in any sense capricious regarding community law. Only that the power between the sexes (that inherited species disequilibrium that culture endlessly medi-ates) was balanced, so producing a confident sauciness in the women and a humorous appreciation in the men.

Later, after I had left them, I came across other Kutchi Rabaris who had settled. Within a generation, the women were in strict purdah, usually a hot compound at the back of a house, where they lived like caged parrots. By day they were bent over in the fields, digging, watched over by the patriarch. Or they worked and cooked in the stifling compound. At night they were locked in. They did not mourn the loss of their freedom, how could they? They had nothing with which to compare their lives. But I could compare them with their still nomadic cousins, whose men looked at them with affection, respect and not a little awe, who could stride out unchaperoned, haggle with shopkeepers and fight with their slings beside their men.

After the decision had been made, women from the other camps came over, bringing gifts of sweets. "This is your dang now, you'll see, you will enjoy living with us."

"But be warned, if you remain with us your skin will become as black as ours. Even your hair will go black."

"We will call you Ratti ben – sister of blood."

"We have no home but these camps. We live under the sky, whether there is sun or rain. The village is not our home, the dang is our home. This is where our property is."

"We are liberal people. We do not judge others but let everyone be."

Then I was shown how to unload my camel, where to peg him, where to place my bed and saddle. We were to spend the night there, beside a brickworks that clanged and banged all night, camped on the rim of a pit of stagnant water and garbage. My translator took off for Rajasthan, and I was left with my new family, with whom I had about five words in common.

There was a sense of urgency getting all the work done by nightfall. The women ran barefoot over stones and thorns chasing the lambs. I tried to help them, but the dogs attacked me as soon as I touched the animals. A little boy, dressed in his fabulously embroidered wedding clothes, pulled me around by the hand, threatening the dogs, trying to explain which lambs belonged to which camp and how to tether them by the neck to the long ropes radiating from each bed. At last it was time to cook, always the same food, twice a day – millet roti and buttermilk soup. Then I climbed onto the mountain of supplies on my bed, lay my head on the saddle, and longed for unconsciousness which arrived around 3 a.m. only to be terminated at five. I was woken by men whistling, clicking, trilling and hooting their music to the flocks. All night they had been on patrol, keeping 5,000 munching, coughing, dust-churning sheep held together in a tight pack (in the midst of which we women and children slept for safety), hitting sticks on the ground and rattling things to scare off thieves, taking turns sleeping on mats on the stones, or giggling at me as I punched and cursed the goats which rubbed themselves against my cot without cease, or sneezed snot all over me.

Each shepherd had slightly different calls, variations on a theme, and the overall effect was something like Amazonian woodwinds with percussion. There were morning calls to move out, a call to bring the sheep to water, and so on. Each man knew his own sheep, which might number in the hundreds, and vice versa, and his particular flock would disentangle itself from the larger flock each morning and follow behind him.

The next day we headed out into rubble and dust. Nothing invited the eye or the soul. The light beat the colour out of everything. Blue became white. Green, a dull grey or dun. Only the women's black withstood the domination of sun, like tiny rents in the sheet of light. The men, in white, merged with sheep and rocks and became invisible. Sometimes we passed other women with their strings of camels. There were many dangs behind and many in front, wave after wave of sheep, millions of them, spilling out of Kutch into the fertile farmlands of Saurashtra. I could not begin to imagine how such a vast movement of men and animals was organised.

The daily routine went something like this. Before first light the women got up and began the day's work. They scoured pots with mud and grit, milked their animals, churned fresh goat milk by hand into buttermilk and ghee, clarified the ghee over a fire, and by then the gears of social intercourse were oiled enough to proceed with the more genial activity of cooking and breakfasting. Tooth-cleaning with a chewing stick followed, then the shepherds would pack some roti in a cloth, take a pannikin for water and lead their flocks off to grazing areas designated by the mukki. Lambs would be put to mothers for a drink, the newborn and the sick kept behind with the women to be transported by camel. Phagu and another man would go off scouting, leaving the camels to feed, guarded by the camel wallah, and the women to sew or walk into nearby towns or villages for supplies. Sometimes we women would wait almost all day, sometimes we would leave in the late mornings, the timings and distances designated by Phagu the night before. Half an hour before leaving time, the unth wallah would bring the camels in, they would be fed a few pieces of roti, then loaded up. Anyone too ill to walk, and you had to be almost dead for that, lay tossing about amid the lambs, groaning like a seasick sailor.

Women, children and the sick would head off with the camels and walk without stopping, sometimes two miles, sometimes thirty, to reach the pre-arranged evening camp. We proceeded in straight lines or crooked ones, depending upon where the walls of cactus and stone – the squares and rectangles of sedentary folks – allowed us.

In the evening, as soon as the unloading was done, some women would go to gather thorn bush for the cooking fires, using a long wooden pole to pick up the sticks, adding them to a pile on their heads, which spread in a tangled mass. Others would walk to the nearest water supply, anything from 200 yards to a couple of miles away, bringing back water on their heads, stacked in three brass pots. Then all started on the cooking.

The flocks would begin pouring out of the ravines. When they arrived in camp, the dust was unendurable. After the lambs had been separated from their mothers and tied to the ropes, after the newborns had been brought to the owners' camps, the camels caught and tethered, after incense had been lit and waved around the outskirts of the dang, when jobs like hafting new sticks, or plaiting new ropes, or drenching the animals, or mending equipment was complete, then, at last, the shepherds could rest with their families — the happiest time of day. They would sit for a while in exhausted silence, then recount the day's events. And the more difficult the day had been, the louder the laughter floating up from the camps.

I had been instructed to teach the children how to read and write, a difficult job given mutual linguistic incomprehension. Education of girls and boys was problematic for mobile people, but it was seen as urgently important for the future. They knew that their way of life could not continue indefinitely, that all their pragmatism, flexibility and skill would not save them from change.

Even so, the dang was a training ground for the children. The little girls had their own pieces of play embroidery and carried small brass pots on their heads. At night they made pretend roti. The smallest boys smoked cigarettes and pipes. Soon these angels would begin leaving camp in the mornings with the men, wrapped in their white turbans, carrying their sticks, calling to the sheep, married and responsible men, earning their own living by the age of eight or nine.

When it became apparent that my teaching skills were as good as my skills as a shepherdess, it was tacitly agreed that I should contribute to the morale of the dang by being Phagu's straight man. If I kept people laughing, then I wasn't a complete waste of space. I never slept more than three hours a night. The animals, packed close around me, scraped themselves against my cot, or bore their young – schloop! – at the foot of it, or coughed or grunted, or leapt up onto my quilt. I whipped at them with a rope in fury. I damaged my elbows and hands punching them. It was anything but funny, I was close to cracking up for lack of sleep, but miming my own nocturnal hysteria was high entertainment for the troops.

When the reality outside our group was so threatening, harmony and light-heartedness within it were essential. It was for this, their use of laughter as a survival tactic, that I most admired them. Especially Phagu, on whom responsibility lay like a cement overcoat. He had to think ahead, plan and worry for them all, knowing that one wrong decision would mean the end of everyone's income. He had to be diplomat, psychologist, hard man, soft man, entrepreneur, spiritual leader, vet, animal handler, negotiator, accountant, husband, father, general and peacekeeper. Men of his calibre are rare in any situation, any culture, and it was clear, whenever he arrived back in camp, his eyes sunk in exhaustion, how much everyone respected and loved him. As did I.

His position was not hereditary. When he began losing his edge or became too old, he would be replaced by a more able man and there would be no loss of face in this. He might continue going on migration under another's leadership, or he might stay at home and send his sons and daughters. But while he was mukki, the community accorded him absolute trust and obedience.

At night he would tell everyone what the following day's route and camp would be, where the water, where the grazing. If there was any change to the plan, he would come back to inform the women. Otherwise they would head in the direction of the agreed place and either catch up with the flocks or enquire. The shepherds would leave special markers to show which way they had gone or to indicate which track not to take. Phagu himself might have to travel many miles ahead and if a bus was available, he took one. Most often he walked.

The first month was so difficult for me that I thought I would have to leave or go mad. After we'd left the open country, we had begun to camp on ploughed fields, where the dust was thick as pitch.

The main income along the way was sheep dung. Phagu would negotiate with a farmer to camp on a particular field. The sheep would eat the stubble and out the other end came fertiliser. The payment would be distributed proportionately among members of the dang, according to the number of sheep each unit had. But even this mutuality in the relationships between mobile and settled was collapsing. Fallow paddocks were declining and farmers were starting to use chemical fertilisers rather than dung.

The weather was stifling hot during the day, and unpleasantly damp at night, because of the irrigated fields nearby. Malaria began to fell the shepherds where they stood. My own body was slimy with fever. Sometimes we went into towns or villages for injections and supplies. Miles along a path, then onto the traffic-congested road, full of fumes and noise and heat.

But the worst thing for me was being stared at wherever I went, sometimes by hundreds of people pushing and shoving at me so that I couldn't breathe. There was nowhere to hide from them. When the Rabari understood how much I hated these crowds, they used their skills to defend me from them. After all, they too were often greeted by children howling "bhoot, bhoot" ("ghost, ghost") when they entered a village.

I found it difficult not to compare the villagers unfavourably with the nomads, who were so much more empathic. The women made up lies on the spot to field the endless questions about me. It entertained them greatly to do so. Sometimes I was a government worker, at others a vet. Once I was a policeman, which really pushed everyone back. And they delivered these fibs with such facility that it was clear that shamming to outsiders was the habit of centuries. But they never lost their capacity for diplomacy, no matter what the provocation.

In the months ahead I never once saw one of them show discourtesy to another human being, no matter how lowly, nor cruelty to another form of life. Although they were proud of themselves as a caste, they seemed to exist somewhere outside the more rigid hierarchies of settled people. They were aware of the air of freedom and liberality surrounding them, it was something they identified as their own, which made them different from (and I'm sure they would tacitly agree, superior to) the peasantry. Even their attitude to religious form was cavalier, notwithstanding the fact that their caste was known for producing great holy men.

Only someone who has sat for six, eight, ten hours on a black ploughed field under a burning sky, day after day, waiting, entirely dependent upon one's inner life, knows the true meaning of boredom. I did not have the nomads' talent for instant slumber, as when, during those infinite afternoons, they put aside their embroidery and snored. I had long since run out of reading material, so the ladies decided I must make my own gudio – stitched mat. We bought all the requisite materials in a little village, then everyone clustered around the pristine white cloth. Parma drew the design, ten women lifted their needles, and off we went. After ten minutes my hands were cramped, but someone would cry out "Karo!" ("Keep going!"). There was a feeling of solidarity, lots of laughter, story-telling, whispered confidences. Women came by from other camps to lend a hand, bringing food. Everything I said in my halting Hindi, Gujarati and sign language, one of the women would turn into a song. Always the same notes and stanza, sung at walking pace with a strong emphasis on the last word.

"Ratti ben's car is coming, it is coming soon, coming *soon*."

"Ratti ben's country is a long way away, long way *away*."

Within a month I had my very own gudio.

Sometimes at night we visited our neighbours' camps for bhajjans – devotional songs. One man would start the first line of a song, his companions joining in. Then the women would begin, huddling together under their black wool, competing with the men, keening their lungs out, giggling when someone got the words wrong or felt a little shy. They sang a song about Ratti ben, my ancient namesake, who had lain between the bodies of two slain men – one a Rabari, the other an enemy (a non-nomad) – to prevent their blood from mixing. They drank tea and sang until the stars swung past midnight. They sang themselves into intoxication.

It was as if they took a spiritual bath in the music, their troubles washed away with songs as old as the Subcontinent. And I was struck once again by their intimacy with each other – the bonds continually strengthened, like calcium laid down in a bone, by singing, or sharing food, or sewing each other's mats, or smoking each other's chillums. They passed through life's storms always with the support of the group, which infused every action and every thought with one voice extending from the time of one's ancestors down through the generations saying, "It is all right. We are all here. There is no such thing as alone."

I wanted to stay with them for a whole year. There was so much to try to understand. I still had no idea, really, how a migration was organised. I had begged Phagu to let me scout with him, but he always refused, saying that it would be dangerous for me, or that I would get tired. He was responsible for my safety. Eventually he relented.

I knew that mukkis often met up to discuss overall tactics, knew that shepherds gathered and disseminated news, but I could not see how it all fitted together to produce these mighty migrations which, far from being chaotic affairs, had more the quality of German machinery. Now I had a chance to witness how it was done.

We walked into a village, out to a farm, across some fields, around a dam, back to the village, across more fields to another dang, up hills, through ravines, made a deal with a farmer, met up with our shepherds and their flocks, and walked back to another farm. That was in the morning. In the afternoon we took a bus to another area altogether.

I watched him out of the corner of my eye. A man unused to sitting still, restless hands, darting eyes. Looking for water, feed, camping places, villages for food and medicine, thinking "... when will the cotton here be harvested, should we risk that jungle area ..." – calculating, observing, comparing, deducing, holding massive amounts of information in the head, juggling it around – the paradigm of human intelligence. This was what nomadism required – resilience, resourcefulness, versatility, flexibility. The capacity to adapt rapidly to changing circumstances, to seize opportunities. And to make connections.

Whenever we came across another grazier, of whatever caste or religion, whether in the bazaar or on a lonely hillside, Phagu would first shake hands with him, then plug in the "lakri o tar" – the walking-stick telegraph.

No shepherd would be seen dead without his stick for leaning on (one leg raised), hitting sheep, fighting gundas or, as one shepherd demonstrated to me, knocking the revolvers out of policemen's hands. It is a symbol for pastoralists everywhere and has given its name to the miraculous networking without which the organisational feat of migration would be impossible. Two pastoralists meet. They shake hands. They swap information. How many sheep in that dang, where is it heading, what are the farmers like in such and such a town, has a certain area been booked by any shepherds from elsewhere, how many sheep have passed through already, what happened on that camel dang, who died on that sheep dang, how much bribe was given to that forest officer, what is the state of the peanut crops in area A, when are the farms in area B harvesting, what did W say to X at village Y regarding how much it cost to get shepherd Z out of that court case, and so on and on. There is some beautiful arithmetic to be understood here, of the permutation/combination kind. So much travelling and meeting increases the chances of cross-fertilisation of information and cross-checking of facts. However, it also increases the likelihood of error, that "noise" which diminishes the effectiveness of any system of information. But there is virtually no noise in the pastoralists' system.

Unlike a game of "Chinese whispers", in which information passed from person to person is changed out of all recognition, the information disseminated by the nomads stays correct down to the finest detail.

It would often be in an individual pastoralist's interest to lie to others who are competing for the same resources. Yet in the larger scheme it is in everyone's interests to stick to the truth. In other words, local personal short-term gain is sacrificed for the greater good, and this among people who have turned dissimulation into an art form.

Sometimes we passed the forts and palaces of Rajputs – the erstwhile rulers in this area. Some were astonishingly beautiful, yet with their crenellated walls, battlements, cannon portals, zenanas and suttee pits, they were also paranoia in stone. Where others might have seen the architectural and artistic triumphs only stratified societies can produce, I saw greed, war, land-grabbing and incarcerated women.

History had swept away the feudal privileges and the maharajahs were having trouble finding the wherewithal to keep their castles standing. Some turned to politics, some turned their palaces into hotels. Most seemed happy to rot quietly in their havelis hoping their sons would do better in business than they had. But the obsession with purdah – the covering and seclusion of women – remained. And although suttee – the ritual of a wife leaping (or being thrown) onto her husband's funeral pyre – was outlawed, it was still thought a fine practice by many modern Rajputs. I had spent enough time in court society to know that it was a field of envy and intrigue. Power was the currency, and everyone vied for it. First sons, the inheritors of title, were treated as potential enemies by their fathers, because they were the most likely to do Daddy in. There were plots, counterplots, shifting alliances, secrets, political scheming, death-threats. And the secondhand power of women in the zenana could be pettily wicked and cruel – the older women breaking the spirit of new daughters-in-law.

How different that way of thinking was from the social structures necessary to the great migrations, which simply could not be accomplished

Never again miss an issue. Subscribe and save.

1 year subscription (4 issues) only $49 (incl. GST). Institutional subscriptions $59. Subscriptions outside Australia $79. All prices include postage and handling.

2 year subscription (8 issues) $95 (incl. GST). Institutional subscriptions $115. Subscriptions outside Australia $155. All prices include postage and handling.

PAYMENT DETAILS Enclose a cheque/money order made out to Schwartz Publishing Pty Ltd. Or; Please debit my credit card (Mastercard, Visa Card or Bankcard accepted).

CARD NO.

EXPIRY DATE   /   AMOUNT $

CARDHOLDER'S NAME

SIGNATURE

NAME

ADDRESS

EMAIL   PHONE

HOW DID YOU HEAR ABOUT QUARTERLY ESSAY? ☐ MEDIA   ☐ WORD OF MOUTH   ☐ ONLINE   ☐ BOOKSHOP/NEWSAGENT

OTHER:

tel 61 3 9654 2000 **fax** 61 3 9654 2290 **email** quarterlyessay@blackincbooks.com **www.quarterlyessay.com**

An inspired gift. Subscribe a friend.

1 year subscription (4 issues) only $49 (incl. GST). Institutional subscriptions $59. Subscriptions outside Australia $79. All prices include postage and handling.

2 year subscription (8 issues) $95 (incl. GST). Institutional subscriptions $115. Subscriptions outside Australia $155. All prices include postage and handling.

PAYMENT DETAILS Enclose a cheque/money order made out to Schwartz Publishing Pty Ltd. Or; Please debit my credit card (Mastercard, Visa Card or Bankcard accepted).

CARD NO.

EXPIRY DATE   /   AMOUNT $

CARDHOLDER'S NAME   SIGNATURE

ADDRESS

EMAIL   PHONE

RECIPIENT'S NAME

RECIPIENT'S ADDRESS

HOW DID YOU HEAR ABOUT QUARTERLY ESSAY? ☐ MEDIA   ☐ WORD OF MOUTH   ☐ ONLINE   ☐ BOOKSHOP/NEWSAGENT

OTHER:

tel 61 3 9654 2000 **fax** 61 3 9654 2290 **email** quarterlyessay@blackincbooks.com **www.quarterlyessay.com**

Delivery Address:
Level 5
289 Flinders Lane
MELBOURNE VIC 3000

No stamp required
if posted in Australia

Quarterly Essay
Reply Paid 79448
MELBOURNE   VIC   3000

- -

Delivery Address:
Level 5
289 Flinders Lane
MELBOURNE VIC 3000

No stamp required
if posted in Australia

Quarterly Essay
Reply Paid 79448
MELBOURNE   VIC   3000

on a ground of deceit. Their success depended upon formal generosity, tolerance and honesty among migrating individuals, families, dangs, castes and religions.

Sometimes at night, when we sat around the cooking fires, I asked questions and struggled to make sense of the replies.

"If the head of a family decides that only one member of that family should go on the dang, then the other brothers and sisters will give that one a fixed wage for grazing the sheep, whether or not he makes any profit. If there is a profit, it will later be distributed among the members of the family."

"But surely this must lead to confusion. What do you do if there are disagreements among yourselves, or with outsiders?"

"There are never fights between or among dangs. No, never. Perhaps a mukki might chastise a younger fellow if he doesn't follow the code and grazes where he shouldn't. But that's all. If there is a police case involving a person of the dang, then the money paid to the police to avoid the case will be paid by all members of the dang."

Everyone participated in these sessions. They loved talking about themselves and were justifiably proud of their expertise. It was always a good excuse to stay up late, share prashad and drink tea. Phagu would lie back on the cot, play with his little daughter (the most adored spoilt brat on earth), teach her songs, then puff on his chillum and stare up at the sky.

"Do you know the stars, Phagu?"

"Oh yes, in times past we Rabari navigated entirely by the stars. We were the pathfinders, which is what our name means. Certain configurations gave the time and place to a very accurate degree. But these days there are watches and the country is settled, so that degree of knowledge is lost."

"How do you think your grandchildren will live? Will they still be nomadic?"

"People tell me there is no future in what I am doing and that I should sell my flocks. But how can I worry about these things now? Grazing the sheep takes all my time and effort and concentration. I'm too concerned with survival, Ratti ben, to answer your deep questions."

Just as in Tibet, the object of the Indian state is to settle the nomads. They are seen as an anachronism, out of tune with the requirements of development. Their way of life is never understood for what it is – a risk-spreading strategy, and a viable alternative to agriculture or wage labour. As recently as 1990, an Indian anthropologist wrote, "The nomads in the present times are a menace to the whole society and their sedentarisation is imperative. With sedentarisation, administration and exercise of control becomes easy." Some of the Rabari are selling their animals and buying trucks, in order to enter the transport business. They see this as a way of retaining a nomadic identity. But of course, once they change occupation, everything else changes as well, and they become indistinguishable from settled people.

As the weather cooled, life became easier for me but harder for them. Now they were susceptible to influenza. More perilous, however, was the fact that the way ahead was constricting, and despite their efforts at good cheer, the atmosphere in camp of an evening was sombre. One day a local caste of herders came and began shouting and threatening us. The women placated them. They sat the men down and gave them biscuits and tea. Yes, we would move on. No need for trouble. After they had gone, everyone joked with me about "war" being imminent and that I'd better learn how to use the stone sling. But the situation was serious and I was given a shepherd's stick, just in case. Phagu was notified to scout another place; the rest of us packed up and walked six miles.

But again, from there, we had to go. Blood had been spilt, despite all the evasive tactics. Phagu had decided that our dang must break up into three groups. Smaller flocks would be less threatening to the locals. So we loaded in silence, and after walking a few miles the line of camels began to split up. Silent, unhappy farewells. That night the dang was miserably reduced, the sadness palpable. We would not see our friends for a long time. From now on, travelling would not only be more physically demanding and dangerous, it would be lonelier as well.

I made the decision to leave them and head back to Jodhpur. They would find the way easier without me. On my last evening on the dang, Phagu's son asked to come with me, to be my driver.

"But I already have a driver and anyway you can't drive."

"You can teach me."

"But why do you want to leave your profession? Is it the money?" It was not the money.

"Well then, is it the difficulty and danger of the work?" No, he did not mind hard work, and he was proud of his skills as a shepherd.

"It is the constant fights and trouble. There is no peace for us night or day. Once we were like kings. Now we are treated like dogs."

In the morning the women came to say goodbye, carrying ceremonial pots on their heads.

Then there were hugs all round, clasped hands and promises of return. I left to the sound of singing.

I have never done anything in my life as demanding as travelling with those people. But I could go back to comfort and security, for them this was real life.

My admiration for them was boundless and while they infuriated me sometimes, I never disliked them. They endured everything without complaint, singing themselves drunk at night or walking twenty extra miles to a temple in order to thank the gods for life. And there was nothing servile about them.

I don't wish to sentimentalise them. They are as capable of underhandedness as anyone in their quest for survival, they are often the bane of peasants trying to protect meagre resources, and their herds and flocks do damage to dwindling forest. But no more than the ploughs and poisons of the farmers and not as much as the venality of the people who exploit them. Something invaluable will be lost if their migrations cease. Because it is the fact of their mobility which strengthens the qualities which so distinguish them – tolerance, wiliness, independence, courage, wit.

Sometimes when it was particularly difficult for me, they would pause in their work to smile, knowingly and kindly, put an arm around my shoulder and say, "Come, drink tea." Or to whisper into the darkness, "Go to sleep, Ratti ben, you are tired out." Words with which they might convey an ambiguous and difficult affection. It was at those moments that the shadow of something remote touched us, fleetingly uniting me with them from across the abyss so that I too could hear the faint echo from our common, immeasurably distant past. "It is all right. We are all here. There is no such thing as alone."

CONCLUSION

The agricultural revolution transformed the earth and changed the fate of humanity. It produced an entirely new mode of subsistence, which remains the foundation of the global economy to this day.

There is no going back. Without human labour hacking at the weeds, or redirecting water, domesticated grains would die out, and without that grain, so would we. The economy which gave us more cheap food, and an increasing population dependent on that food, provided no exit other than famine.

When *Homo sapiens sapiens* inherited the earth, we numbered perhaps a third of a million. Around 10,000 years ago, we had increased to perhaps three million, and by the time farming had given rise to civilisation 5,000 years ago, there might have been up to twenty million of us in the world. We are now six billion and rising.

By requiring us to become sedentary, agriculture changed the way we conceive of our place in nature, and it changed the way we distribute goods. In pre-agricultural societies social structures were more or less egalitarian and food was shared. Population was limited. Injustice and subjugation did not begin with settlement (one only need look at Jane Goodall's work with chimps to know that murderousness is a primate inheritance), but they found a rich habitat there in which to flourish.

The process of agricultural takeover of hunter-gatherer economies has almost reached its conclusion. In 10,000 BC all human beings were hunters and gatherers; by 1,500 AD this had reduced to about 1 per cent. And by the mid-twentieth century, it was down to 0.001 per cent.

What damage do we cause ourselves when the earliest extant efforts of the human mind to find its place in the universe have gone, never to be recovered?

And now the more recent forms of nomadism – pastoralism and artisanship – are also being brought to a halt. They do not fit well with modernising drives. Such nomads are difficult to control and tax, independent-minded, skeptical, and they tend to value knowledge above accumulated wealth.

Agriculture set us on a path to the urban and industrial revolutions, and finally to the wild consumerism of late capitalism. Like those previous chapters of the agricultural story, post-industrial globalisation is achieving material wealth, longer life, greater choice. But it cannot distribute those benefits. The rate at which the gap between over- and under-privileged is widening depends on which statistics you read, but no one seriously doubts that it is widening, both within and between countries. Evidence from its own institutions indicates that a couple of billion people suffer from chronic malnutrition and live in poverty.

Most importantly, the generation of that wealth requires an increasing pillage of the environment. Global warming alone should be terrifying enough to galvanise us into changing habits of consumption. It does not appear to be doing so. Four billion years of life on earth. Millions of those years reigned over by the dinosaurs. Us lot a mere 200,000-year blip and according to several commentators, including Lord Rees, the UK Astronomer Royal, we are not looking good to get through the next hundred years, let alone compete with the dinosaurs.

One of the questions we need to ask, if we're to have a future, is "Where, when, in what situations, did we cause less damage to ourselves, to our environment, and to our animal kin?" One answer is: when we were nomadic. It was when we settled that we became strangers in a strange land, and wandering took on the quality of banishment. Pilgrimage – religious or secular – remained as a relic of the hunting and foraging life.

There can be no return to previous modes of living, no retreat to the traditional as a way of shoring up identity, or denying rationality and the benefits of science. Such retrogression only lands us in kitsch. But there might be ways into previous kinds of thinking. Pilgrimages, let's say, to newly imagined territories where, instead of arrogantly dismissing the traditional as useless to modernity, the best of each might be integrated.

When Adam Smith talked about the "wealth of nations", he wasn't referring simply to money, but to a whole ensemble of requirements to wellbeing. Perhaps, who knows, the materialist progress we have made since urbanisation, and the values existing before it, could meld into some marvellous, unprecedented syncretism. But if that is too much to expect, at least attention to nomadic modes of thinking might get us closer to finding whatever solutions to the disintegrations of modern life are actually available to us.

So what are the qualities that nomadic cultures tend to encourage? It seems to me that they are the humanistic virtues. The world is approached as a series of complex interactions, rather than simple oppositions, connecting pathways rather than obstructive walls. Nomads are comfortable with uncertainty and contradiction. They are cosmopolitan in outlook, because they have to deal with difference, negotiate difference. They do not focus on long-term goals so much as continually accommodate themselves to change. They are less concerned with the accumulation of wealth and more concerned with the accumulation of knowledge. The territorial personality – opinionated and hard-edged – is not revered. Tolerance, which accommodates itself to things human and changeable, is. Theirs are Aristotelian values of "practical wisdom" and balance. Adaptability, flexibility, mental agility, the ability to cope with flux. These traits shy away from absolutes, and strive for an equilibrium that blurs rigid boundaries.

There are people whose faith in technology is strong enough for them to believe that there are no limitations on us as a species. We will colonise other planets, or find new sources of energy. Our big brains will save us. Others take the gloomy view that we are hardwired for disaster, that wherever we've been, we've destroyed our environment, and we will always do so. Coded into this view is the tacit belief that our fate is determined by our genes, and our brains, far from saving us, are the very organs that have become an evolutionary disadvantage, because we are using them to destroy the resources on which we live – that is, the planet.

It is an irony of our times that while classical nomadism is ending, hypermobility has become the very hallmark of modernity. It is creating the largest shifts of population the world has ever witnessed. Tribes of labourers on the margins of world capitalism, refugees fleeing wars and ethnic cleansing, rural economic and ecological refugees draining into cities – all these constitute a wandering nation of a hundred million desperate people. Migration is the quintessential experience of our time, and has become the most contentious issue of contemporary politics.

At one end of the spectrum, those hundred million victims of history; at the opposite end, wealthy people enjoying an almost unrestricted freedom of movement. Business executives commuting intercontinentally between home and work; tourists supporting whole economies in underdeveloped countries or buying apartments on vast cruise ships that never dock. And increasingly, there are people like me, who live in several countries, have complex identities and feel allied to more than one culture. We live in what Edward Said called "a generalised condition of homelessness". These new forms of nomadism will shape the culture of the new century in unpredictable ways.

For one thing, they raise questions concerning personal and national identity. The political constructs of homeland, nationhood, patriotism came into being because of a yearning to belong to a spiritual geography. In the nineteenth century, "the nation" seemed a stable, unambiguous entity. But what can such constructs mean in this turbulent, increasingly placeless world where people are forever crossing borders and hybridising?

The paradox is that the new nomadism of the rich is inherently antithetical to the older forms it is replacing. A traditional nomad had an exquisite understanding of her environment. Hers was a peripatetic sense of place, based on the body's rhythm, sensually tuned in to the surroundings, and constantly connecting her with others along the pathways. For her there was "no such thing as alone". The modern nomad is not just uprooted from place, but severed from deep connections with other human beings. Local attachments are the same as all other attachments — shallow. Kinship and community bonds become frail and brittle. Not so much a nomad, as a monad.

This is the price paid for a freedom of movement based entirely on whim and wealth. A forgetting of the interconnectedness of all things. "To be rooted is perhaps the most important and least recognised need of the human soul," wrote Simone Weil in 1942. If that is true, then the new nomadism is contributing to modernity's malaise.

Emile Durkheim's study of suicide found that people who had fewer social connections, bonds and obligations were more likely to kill themselves. The more connected we are, the less likely we are to give way to despair. Beyond a basic level of comfort, money makes no difference to that despair.

Detachment from our surroundings is becoming increasingly "normal". We move through the world faster and faster, looking at it, but not being in it. And the more mobile we become, the less sense we have of being sensually enmeshed with our world and interdependent with, responsible for, others. The ultimate version of this placeless, isolated individual is the virtual nomad, plugged into a computer terminal. On the screen, a virtual earth full of trees, birds and butterflies. Outside the window, a wasteland. Staying "in touch" has become purely conceptual.

For us here in Australia, it has been easy to overlook ecological problems, protected as we are by our precarious good luck, but that is changing, and changing faster than predicted. We have managed in just 200 years to bugger up our country, to cut an ever-widening swathe through its natural resources. The famine, drought and political chaos that we hear of in places like Africa are not temporary aberrations, they are systemic. When the desertification and the salination and the loss of species and the lack of water can no longer be ignored, will such chaos extend out to us, the privileged?

Old Aboriginal people are worried too, by droughts and decreasing bush tucker, but they see this as a natural consequence of being torn away from their ritual duties. There has been such a ripping asunder of their relationships to sacred sites over the years, it is only to be expected that "orphaned" country will be ill and unproductive. Aboriginal people see their role as keeping country and its vitality in trust for all life to come. Other Australians might do well to find ways of sharing that role.

I shall probably be accused of romanticism. (Romanticism: the desire to escape reality rather than apprehend it better.) Or for idealising pre-modern times out of an ignorance of its hardships. But that is not at all my intention. For one thing, I would have died at age twelve without modern medicine. And I should think contemporary Aborigines might baulk at a return to the foraging life, particularly now as the ravages of drought eradicate the last vestiges of the possibility of that method of subsistence. And I would be more than happy to see the benefits of science – good health, less grinding worry, longer life – brought to the Himalayan peasants.

Nor do I think nomads are or ever were greenies in the way we understand that term today. Their cultural practices, like cultural practices everywhere, could become destructive in new settings, and were often slow to change. And Dreamings could be violent and vengeful. Nevertheless, cultures based on mobility require the collection, memorising and integration of observations of environmental processes, knowledge systems that over time become encoded into cosmologies.

And one does not have to be a romantic to be in awe of the Dreaming – that marvellous, moving and all-encompassing poem to life.

CODA

In every religion I can think of, there exists some variation on the theme of abandoning the settled life and walking one's way to godliness. The Hindu Sadhu, leaving behind family and wealth to live as a beggar; the pilgrims of Compostela walking away their sins; the circumambulators of the Buddhist kora; the Hajj. What could this ritual journeying be but symbolic, idealised versions of the foraging life? By taking to the road we free ourselves of baggage, both physical and psychological. We walk back to our original condition, to our best selves. "House life is crowded and dusty," said the Buddha. "Life gone forth is wide open. It is not easy, living in a household, to lead a Holy Life as utterly perfect and pure as a polished shell. Suppose I shaved off my hair and beard, put on the yellow cloth, and went forth from the house life into homelessness."

Anna Clark

It is a difficult task to write a response to Inga Clendinnen — she is a hard act to follow. Yet her essay *The History Question* raises important questions about teaching Australian history in schools. And, unlike so much of the history wars in recent years, it has begun a conversation that invites engagement and response.

The Prime Minister is right to be worried about low levels of historical interest among young Australians. When I interviewed a Year 12 student in Darwin earlier this year, she said that she would rather learn any history than her own nation's: "I remember doing it heaps in primary school and it was really boring, and it still is, and Australian history just makes me want to cry. It's so boring and I can't stand it." Her view is by no means universal, but it's clear that something needs to be done if the perception that Australian history is boring prevents students from learning it.

Yet the answer cannot be to promote national pride at the expense of critical engagement with the subject. In 2004 the then Education Minister, Brendan Nelson, insisted that Australian children be taught national values and that schools install a "functioning flagpole" to fly the nation's flag. In Howard's Australia Day speech this year, he criticised the failure to teach Australian history as an "objective record of achievement".

The problem here is not about whether to teach the nation's past, but how to teach it. History should not be about nation-building, as Clendinnen rightly insists, but if it's taught well it can help to build a better nation:

> I would like students at every level to study Australian history because I believe that one of the best ways to "teach values" is to exercise minds by engaging them in investigation of conflicts between competing values and interests, always with a proper regard for clarity and justice of analysis and the relevance of evidence.

To be sure, students themselves want to engage with the past and examine different readings of it. They don't want a dry recounting of events – they know that history is much more than that. They also don't want parochial history; they want to learn about Australia's place in the world and how Australia's history compares with the histories of other nations.

In the lead-up to the centenary of Federation in 2001, for example, significant public anxiety was expressed by politicians, historians and educationists that young Australians were oblivious to their own country's foundation. Following the massive government-sponsored campaign to increase awareness of Federation, many more students were able to name Australia's first prime minister. But is that all history is?

A Year 11 student from Brisbane who recalled the centenary celebrations thought that there should be more to the subject than just being able to remember Edmund Barton: "Like I know the name of the first prime minister, but that's the only prime minister I really know, Edmund Barton, and I don't know anything about him, I just know his name. And I don't know anything about any of the other prime ministers."

It is not enough to just learn "the facts", and students are already telling us this. They understand the importance of studying what it means to be Australian, but only as long as the story they learn is not narrowly simplistic. Another student from Brisbane agreed that Australian history should be compulsory, but if it is, "It shouldn't be inward-looking like America, and I think it should be the whole investigative sort of history. I don't like the idea of just learning facts, and then being told what to think."

Clendinnen writes that "history's social utility depends on it being cherished as a critical discipline, and not as a tempting source of gratifying tales" – so it is essential that it be taught in all its complexity. As history educationists such as Tony Taylor and Carmel Young have stressed, "History education is about the development of 'historical literacy' rather than a simplistic notion that history is about the recall of historical facts or, at best, an entertaining story." Knowledge of the past is a critical component of historical literacy, they maintain, but so too is the ability to understand multiple perspectives, develop research skills and form arguments.

That means we need students who can read the past, who can evaluate historical sources, distinguish different voices, and interrogate its stories. And then they need to be able to write the past. The task extends beyond simply transmitting "what happened" to teaching students to engage critically with the subject. (Because doing it badly, as we have seen regarding Japan's persistent denialism, has terrible moral implications for the way nations face up to their collective past.)

In other words, we need to teach students to *do* history: to constantly reconcile judging the past from our own present values and empathising with people from another age; to understand how historical interpretations change over time; and to consider different points of view.

And for that a great deal of professional development and funding is required. If history is to have integrity in schools, it needs to be supported – and by this I don't mean flagpole subsidies, but actual professional development, for teachers and resources in the *classroom*.

This debate presents a great opportunity to cement the place of Australian history in school, but it's essential that it be done well. If it is, we can hope that students might learn to practise history as Clendinnen herself has done with such timely consideration.

Anna Clark

Alan Atkinson

Inga Clendinnen's essay offers an intriguing and powerful argument about the way genuine History works. I'm not sure that she really answers the question as to who owns the past. Maybe we can use a kind of Lockean logic and say that whoever makes historical understanding most fruitful is the true owner. But it's more interesting to wonder why such a question should be asked at all. Probably, it's just another way of asking who owns the present and the future.

Of course, "contest" is one of the favourite words of current debate in the humanities. In earlier times, such as the 1960s and '70s, the equivalent was "struggle", a word with Marxist connotations – although when Marx himself was writing, "struggle" was part of Darwinian thinking, as in "the struggle for existence". Somehow, we are attuned now to the idea that the human past was a kind of game, more virtual than real, so that "contest" seems more fitting. The more urgent reality now is in the way historians fight things out among themselves. No doubt this is partly a result of the impact of journalism on scholarship, which makes delicate and complex disagreements into prize-fights.

In these circumstances, Clendinnen's argument is certainly a breath of fresh air. When I was about two-thirds through my teaching career, I convinced myself that most undergraduates, when they start learning history, don't really believe in the distinct reality of the past. Without concentrated effort and without trained or self-trained imagination, it is often too hard to comprehend the existence of human beings through long periods of time different from our own. A proper intellectual grasp of remoteness and of distance, whether of time or space, is difficult enough in itself. It is something which began to be attempted by the mass of educated people in the nineteenth century. Taking on board the lived experience of human beings fundamentally like – but also fundamentally unlike – oneself in such faraway circumstances is even harder.

The task of teaching and of writing history is to persuade students and readers that the past is equally real with the present.

The current campaign against academic history is peculiarly depressing because it seeks to undermine the intellectual and imaginative process central to this effort, which is the hard work of generations. It is an attack on the whole purpose of historical research and training. In this respect, it's surprising that Clendinnen doesn't explore the current complex, frequently fertile but often acrimonious relationship between scholarship and journalism. Journalists come in many kinds, with many points of view, and no doubt it's wrong to think that the history wars are simply a "contest" between scholarship and journalism. However, journalism is not much concerned about the long term, except insofar as it can be immediately related to the present. Its intellectual methodology is intricate and important, but it is therefore radically different from that of academic history. And yet journalism now seeks to set the standard for history writing – sometimes deliberately and explicitly. And it has the upper hand because it is much more closely attuned to the needs of the market.

Clendinnen's discussion of historical fiction, however, is spot-on. It's extraordinary, and surely symptomatic of larger movements of thought, that someone so highly literate as Kate Grenville should have such a superficial and negative understanding of the purposes of academic history. Her statement, quoted by Clendinnen, that historical scholarship is an intellectual and never an imaginative process, has no basis in truth. It suggests an almost wilful blindness in reading the best work of historians. In July, at a conference in Canberra, I heard another equally famous writer of historical fiction suggest (to an audience of historians!) that they were geologists when it came to understanding the past, whereas people like himself were artists. How is it possible, among a population more highly educated than any other since the world began, for the understanding of scholarship in the humanities to be so impoverished?

It may be that academic historians are badly out of step with the times. If so, in the long-term interests of good scholarship we need to be able to convince ourselves that, at least occasionally, the times are out of step with us. Clendinnen is an historian of unusual ability, and her essay is a crucial reminder of what the discipline at its best stands for. The past, as she says, is a very strange place. Understanding it in anything like a satisfactory way calls not only for prodigious quantities of accurate information. It also depends on sustained and rigorous imaginative effort. It requires a difficult balance between sympathy and detachment, and, on top of that (as Clendinnen makes beautifully clear), an understanding that there are some aspects of the human experience which it is impossible to penetrate.

At the same time, there is one remark in the essay very hard to agree with. Novelists, she says, have one advantage over historians. They can relay conversations, whereas "historians can't do conversations at all". Ejaculations and last words they can manage, such as "Liberty or death" and "Such is life." Also, she says, "They can sometimes make monologues out of formal speeches or secret diaries or confessional statements. But the informal verbal interactions of daily life? No," she concludes. "They are lost to us." And yet, in my own university library there is shelf after shelf of recorded dialogue from the past – trial proceedings, parliamentary debates, question-and-answer evidence before official inquiries. Maybe in many cases these are only roughly symptomatic of "the informal verbal interactions of daily life", but to say that this fundamental aspect of the human past is "lost to us" seems perverse. Also, where does this leave the massive literature on oral history?

In fact, we know a vast amount about "the informal verbal interactions of daily life" in the past. Interpreting it and presenting it in a way that makes sense in the present, and as dialogue, is another matter. But in fact, this is precisely the kind of intellectual challenge that, as Clendinnen says herself, is central to historical scholarship. The strangeness and self-sufficiency of the past is nowhere more obvious than in the conversations its inhabitants had with each other, free of any sense that their remote descendants might be listening in. Similarly, the intricate difficulty of writing well about the past is nowhere more painful than when we try to decode what we hear, especially when there are two or more voices in play. Clendinnen might have presented an even stronger case for the human importance of good history had she not suggested that this part of the job is not worth the effort.

Alan Atkinson

John Hirst

I agree with much in *The History Question*, especially the strictures on Kate Gren-ville and her *Secret River* and the doubts about supplying schoolchildren with a single narrative history of Australia. Not surprisingly, I do not agree with Clendinnen's strictures on my essay "How Sorry Can We Be?", which I pub-lished recently in *Sense & Nonsense in Australian History*.

A strange fate has befallen me. Inga Clendinnen, the brilliant interpreter of deeds and words in the past, misunderstands me, alive, now, in Melbourne. When she deals with the opening of my essay, she misunderstands both me and Rudyard Kipling.

In response to an Australian critic of the misdeeds of the British Empire, Kipling gave an opinion which I endorsed:

> A man might just as well accuse his father of a taste in fornication
> (citing his own birth as an instance) as a white man mourn over
> his land's savagery in the past.

Clendinnen interprets Kipling to be saying that "the child, the issue of the fornication, having had no voice in the business of his making, is born 'clean'". He is not saying that. He is saying that your origins lie in dirty deeds, but you cannot regret or be sorry for them because without them you would not exist where you now do. Or, as I put it after the quotation: "The critic only exists because of the deed he criticises." Clendinnen's misunderstanding of this point throws out her whole assessment of my essay.

I identified two attacks on the Aborigines: the first which deprived them of their land and the second which deprived them of their civil rights. The first was the action of British settlers; the second of the Australian nation. Because the second was a gratuitous act of the nation is one reason why I think it should be apologised for. Clendinnen then takes me to be saying that I am not willing to apologise for the first attack because it was not the deed of the nation. In fact I say the opposite: because it was not the work of the nation is not a let-out. We might be tempted, I say, to shift the blame to the British settlers, but we cannot because we are the beneficiaries of their deeds. Here are the two passages in question (mine and hers) so that readers can see how Clendinnen's initial misunderstanding makes her incapable of giving a fair account of my subsequent views.

Hirst:

> So why does the second attack on the Aborigines warrant an apology and the first one not? Though the High Court judges in Mabo spoke of the Australian nation expropriating the Aborigines, this is not so. The settlers were English, Irish and Scots who invaded Aboriginal lands with the sanction of the British state. Only subsequently was the Australian nation formed by those settlers and their children. It is true that the nation was only made possible by this expropriation, which is why I consider it cannot be apologised for. Some might be tempted to point the finger at the British, but settler Australians are the beneficiaries of their deeds. The second attack on the Aborigines was an attack by the Australian nation (though the agents were the various state governments) in pursuit of a national ideal. I accept what Rai Gaita has argued that if a nation can feel pride at its past achievements it can properly feel shame (though not guilt) for its past misdeeds. Forcibly removing Aboriginal children was undoubtedly a misdeed. What finally makes the case for apology compelling in this instance is that some of the victims are still alive.

Clendinnen:

> Hirst argues there can be no apology for the first attack: the conquest. Why not? Because that first offence was committed not by "Australians", but by "the settlers ... English, Irish and Scots who invaded Aboriginal lands with the sanction of the British state. Only subsequently was the Australian nation formed by those settlers and their children." The nation made possible by that expropriation is not implicated in the injury, therefore the nation cannot apologise.

By contrast, "the second attack was an attack by the Australian nation … in pursuit of a national ideal."

Why I do not want to apologise for the first attack is made clear at the opening of the essay with the Kipling quotation. Here I repeat the point: "the nation was only made possible by this expropriation, which is why I consider it cannot be apologised for." Clendinnen, not understanding that point, renders it as: "The nation made possible by that expropriation is not implicated in the injury, therefore the nation cannot apologise." *Not implicated in the injury* is her misreading. Of course settler Australians are implicated in the original injury. Our dilemma, as I see it, is that we cannot disown it.

From these misreadings comes Clendinnen's supposition that I accept no obligations to the Aborigines arising from the original dispossession. Since I told her this was a misreading (for this public argument continues what began in private), she now adds: "I could well have him wrong here but this is what his words say to me."

My words on this matter in this essay were:

> A position of hard realism about the nation resting on conquest certainly does not require that we abandon sympathy for Aborigines as fellow humans. We must understand what Aborigines have experienced since 1788 if any policy-making in Aboriginal affairs is to be effective.

In the previous essay in *Sense & Nonsense in Australian History*, I wrote:

> Australians owe a moral debt to the Aborigines. It is determined by the standards we set ourselves today and the current position of the Aborigines. It does not depend on a condemnation of the first Europeans who settled the country, just as our compensatory action cannot be directed to restoring the status quo ante.

The penultimate essay in the collection is a critique of current policy in Aboriginal affairs and recommendations for improvement.

With all this evidence to hand I am puzzled at Clendinnen's giving any space to a supposition of my heartlessness and indifference.

The worst offence in the second attack on the Aborigines was the removal of Aboriginal children from their mothers. I wrote:

This was cold-blooded cruelty planned by a distant Bureau in pursuit of the ideal of racial purity. Humankind has been very inventive in its cruelty, but cruelty of this sort did not appear until the early twentieth century. We are still struggling to come to terms with it.

Clendinnen quarrels with this, saying that "it is difficult to recall a more bureaucratised cruelty than that exercised, with chilling dispassion, by the Spanish Inquisition." I did intend all the words in my sentence to count. The Inquisition might be allowed to be a bureaucracy, but it did not operate at a distance from its victims and it certainly was not pursuing racial purity. The pursuit of racial purity is a special cruelty because the victims are identified not by their deeds, their words, their allegiances or their location, but by their blood. They cannot escape – unlike the targets of the Inquisition, who could recant their views. Clendinnen completes what she takes to be a refutation of this passage by saying "Humans have always been good at cruelty" and so echoes my own remark: "Humankind has been very inventive in its cruelty."

Clendinnen wants to resist my identification of two attacks – and two moral responses to them. If the second attack was the work of the nation, how, she asks, can I be certain when the nation came into being? I seem to be adopting a "remarkably crisp periodisation". Of course national consciousness rose unevenly, but the second attack on the Aborigines is prima facie evidence of its existence. A minority of Aboriginal natives was not an anomaly in British colonies; they were a threat to a nation that conceived of itself as young, pure, fresh and white.

The first attack on the Aborigines was necessarily violent. I insisted on this as against what I called the liberal fantasy, the belief that the Aborigines could have been expropriated nicely if only there had been better communication or a treaty. Clendinnen criticises my approach on the ground that it avoids the moral difference between those settlers who were killers and those who were not. There were differences in approach by the settlers, which do interest me. Broadly there were two options: drive the Aborigines off the run or bring them to headquarters and make them dependents. But there are difficulties in making moral judgments as between settlers. Notice that they all believe that they have the right to invade and seize Aboriginal land, which one way or another will usually lead to Aboriginal violence, which someone has to cope with if settlement is to remain secure.

Clendinnen is interested in the choices settlers made. So consider: a squatter chooses not to be a killer; but what will happen when this choice runs up against his choice to make money by running sheep on Aboriginal land? There were squatters who never killed, but there are not many records of squatters frustrated by Aboriginal violence giving up the enterprise. The thing about the frontier is that decent men end up doing indecent things. How much killing they end up doing will depend on chance or circumstances that they do not control or do not understand. The well-disposed settler may unknowingly make camp on a sacred site; he might think it right to reward only those Aborigines who work for him and resist the demands of the rest: both these actions are likely to lead to trouble. His shepherd might be speared because he took the Aboriginal woman offered to him without realising that he now had incurred obligations to her kin. The Aborigines think the spearing has settled the matter; the squatter thinks the Aborigines must be taught a lesson. Across cultures proper behaviour does not have the usual consequences. Morality gets tricky for the participants and for us. The lore of the hard or hardened men on the frontier said that settlers who treated Aborigines well could still be attacked by them – which we can understand to be true.

It is a relief to be treating a subject where there is genuine difference between us, but odd for me to be reminding Clendinnen about the complexities of culture clash, on which she is an expert. Her concern here for moral judgment and looking at particular cases is leading her in the direction of liberal fantasy – if all the settlers had decided not to be killers, then the conquest would have occurred without killing. I don't think so.

John Hirst

Correspondence

Geoffrey Bolton

In her stimulating essay, Inga Clendinnen enters the debate as to whether authors of fiction offer more penetrating insights into the past than historians confined to evidence open to testing. She concludes that good novelists "widen our sense of what humans might be capable. Historians are concerned with what men and women have actually done." This works well enough when writer and reader share cultural perspectives. Novelists such as Eleanor Dark and Kate Grenville or a modern historian like Inga Clendinnen can offer admirably convincing reconstructions of the interactions of Englishmen and Koori in early New South Wales. But some societies, such as the fifteenth-century Aztecs, are so alien in their cultural preconceptions as to baffle empathy. They can't be written out of history, but they offer intractable challenges to both historians and novelists working in the early twenty-first century.

In my experience the difficulties do not end there. Consider the following. Some years ago a senior Cambridge historian acted as external examiner for a Ph.D. thesis written by a Sudanese candidate on the subject of nineteenth-century British imperialism. In exposing the shortcomings of British imperial practice the student made considerable use of the published memoirs of General Sir Harry Flashman VC (1822–1915). The candidate's methodology was impeccable. His use of quotations was apt and accurate. Unfortunately he had failed to realise that the Flashman memoirs are a spoof. They are the work of a modern novelist, George MacDonald Fraser, who discovered Flashman as the school bully in that popular Victorian classic *Tom Brown's Schooldays*. Fraser decided to imagine his subsequent career. In his hands Flashman becomes a liar, a lecher and a coward, as well as a bully, his only redeeming features his skill for languages and his cheerfully cynical realism, but his luck carries him to fame, wealth and professional success. Fraser buttresses his fictions with a good deal of respectable research, so that Flashman's adventures in the Crimean War, the

Indian Mutiny and elsewhere are compatible with what contemporary writers and later historians tell us about these events. It was thus understandable that the Sudanese postgraduate failed to detect the inauthenticity of his source. The thesis was referred back for rewriting. Of course, the student might have argued that the Flashman novels give a more penetrating and lively account of nineteenth-century imperialism than any amount of history confined to ascertainable facts; but apparently he accepted the verdict docilely.

Some are less docile, and would protest against asserting the superiority of Western traditions of historiography. In a refereed journal, *Studies in Western Australian History* (no. 22), Neville Green, a veteran historian of Aboriginal–settler relations, was taken to task by a young historian for failing to give the same credence to Nyoongar folklore as to written and printed sources. Rottnest, now an island holiday resort off Fremantle, was used from 1838 to 1931 as a prison for Aborigines, many of them deported from their home country for spearing sheep and cattle. The Nyoongar story claims that a guillotine was set up on the jetty at Rottnest, and that every time a new contingent of prisoners arrived a man was decapitated in order to show the newcomers the penalty for misbehaviour. By all the criteria of conventional historical research there are problems about this story. There is no evidence of a Rottnest guillotine in any written source: nothing in the archives in Perth or London, no eyewitness accounts, no newspaper reports, no mention by even so assiduous a chronicler of Aboriginal maltreatment as the Reverend John Gribble. I can't believe it.

The story of the Rottnest guillotine, however, has some value as a fiction showing how some Aboriginal people regarded their dispossession and imprisonment, but that puts it in a different genre from historical writing. It stands in the same light as the stories about Captain Cook and Ned Kelly told by the Gurindji and other Victoria River people, as recorded by Deborah Bird Rose. Nobody would use these materials as evidence for biographies of Cook or Kelly, but it is fascinating to learn how Cook becomes transformed into the first of the bad whitefellas who took the land without negotiating for it, and Kelly is seen as the good whitefella who supported and taught the Aboriginal people. Trouble arises when this kind of storytelling becomes conflated with the known events of history.

A classic example is the Forrest River incident of 1926. Reducing the accepted facts to a bare outline: a Kimberley pastoralist who had taken up land recently excised from an Aboriginal reserve was fatally speared. Two policemen and a posse of civilians went in search of his killer, but failed to find him (though he was later arrested and imprisoned). Allegations spread that the party shot a number of unoffending Aborigines and burnt the bodies. A royal commissioner found that around a dozen victims met their deaths at the hands of the party. The two constables were arrested, but a magistrate held that the evidence was insufficient for prosecution. Most historians accepted the royal commission's account, but Rod Moran in *Massacre Myth* argues that there were no killings, the allegations arising out of the overheated imagination of the local Anglican missionary. This has led to ongoing controversy, further complicated because Aboriginal oral history places the death toll at more than a hundred, and this figure received endorsement from the very considerable authority of Greg Dening in a review in the *Australian's Review of Books* in 1998. Personally I find it impossible to accept the larger figure for several reasons, but I realise that I lay myself open to an accusation of denying the Kimberley Aborigines ownership of their past. The question is further complicated because, even within the canons of Western historiography, there is a great gulf between Dening's acceptance of indigenous oral tradition and Windschuttle's scepticism, but both can claim respectable academic precedents. It is hard to carry the debate further when there is no agreement about acceptable methodology.

Australian historians are not the only ones to be confronted by demands that indigenous epistemology should be accorded the same respect as the conventions of mainstream history. There have been similar movements in North America and New Zealand. It is arguable that Australian historians are not paying enough attention to the ensuing debates. Perhaps other questions might be asked. How do contemporary historians in Mexico treat the Aztecs? (After all, generations of English schoolchildren have been reminded that 2,000 years ago their ancestors painted themselves with woad and burnt their enemies in wicker cages.) I follow Clendinnen in discriminating between parables set in the past by storytellers in any culture (Tolstoy, Grenville, the Nyoongar elders) and histories constrained by tested rules of evidence. If historians can never achieve Ranke's goal of rediscovering the past as it actually was, we must take pains to avoid demonstrable error. Storytellers are under no such constraint. They can and should use the materials of the past to offer their audiences insights into the human condition, but we must not call them history.

Geoffrey Bolton

Mark McKenna

On 12 October, I was fortunate enough to share a platform with Inga Clendinnen. We were "in conversation" at Gleebooks in Sydney. Sitting with Inga on stage, I could appreciate her ability to communicate with an audience. Clendinnen has developed a devoted readership not only because of her prose, which is always "in conversation" with her readers, but also because of her ability to perform her history. At Gleebooks she held the audience spellbound as she recited some of the more memorable stories from her recent work. Inga Clendinnen's success in reaching out to a public audience demonstrates that there is a substantial and broadly based readership for Australian history. Despite the gloomy future for academic history diagnosed by some of Australia's major publishers, many readers want history based on both powerful narrative and scholarly rigour.

One of the first questions I asked Inga related to the resurgence of Anzac Day over the last decade or more. As she writes in *The History Question*, her views on Anzac Day differ from mine. She is more optimistic, believing that the "elasticity" of the Gallipoli legend will "confound" any manipulation on the part of our political leaders. This is how we discussed the issue on 12 October:

"Inga, I'd like to move now to your thoughts on the resurgence of Anzac Day. Before I get to the politics of this, I wanted to ask you if you'd share with us the story of your personal relationship to Anzac Day. There is a wonderful section at the beginning of the essay where you try to explain your affection for the day through your memories of attending the Dawn Service in Geelong with your father in the late 1930s. I wonder if I could ask you to read those few paragraphs to us."

Inga then told the story of how, as a young girl, she was smuggled by her father into the Dawn Service at Johnstone Park in Geelong. He had fought on the Western Front. She spoke of her memory of the men who stood around her, their stoic silence, the intensity of their emotions, the sound of the lone bugle at dawn, a memory that always sweeps her back into "that strange blend of emotions – pride, grief, anger – as if it were yesterday".

This is the story of Inga Clendinnen's childhood memories of Anzac Day, and it is powerfully told. But it is also a personal and emotional connection with Anzac Day that I do not share. My memories of Anzac Day were shaped more by the new politics of the 1960s and 1970s, a time when there was a vigorous debate about the commemoration of Anzac Day. Clendinnen's affection for the solemn rituals of the Dawn Service is deeply felt, part of the very fabric of her identity, and it goes a long way towards explaining her optimism concerning the recent resurgence of Anzac Day. For me, that resurgence is worrying, and while I do not claim to understand fully the elevated status of Anzac Day in John Howard's Australia, I'd offer a more critical account of it than the one put forward in *The History Question*.

I despair at the crass commercialisation of 25 April. Take the recent Anzac Day Dawn Services at Gallipoli, the voice of John Laws booming out over Anzac Cove as the Ode is read, rock videos playing, young Australians standing wrapped in the flag, stubbies in hand, beer bottles and waste strewn on the ground afterwards (is this the MCG or Anzac Cove?). To me, this cheap choreography, much of it encouraged by the state, is not "sober mourning" but an example of the new Australian patriotism – largely unreflective and blind to its political exploitation.

The fact that we now seem to have lost the ability to debate Anzac Day, that it has become an article of national faith and communion, a kind of sacred parable we dare not question, is another indication of the narrowing of political debate in Australia. We seem to have lost our critical faculties when it comes to the One Day of the Year. With politicians tripping over one another to praise the fallen heroes, and media outlets whipping up patriotic fervour, the day has become more holy than 25 December. The history of Australia's invasion of Turkey in 1915 as part of the British Empire (remember the Empire?) has been airbrushed from public memory. Anzac Day has been emptied of its historical context and is now remembered as a story of Aussies coming valiantly of age (yet again!). As one pilgrim told an ABC journalist at the Gallipoli Dawn Service last Anzac Day, "It's not about the Empire, it's about us." All of these things suggest that the Anzac myth is certainly capable of "elasticity", as Clendinnen writes, but they also suggest that for many Australians it has become less about "sober mourning" and more about feelgood flag-waving.

Inga Clendinnen believes that no amount of government direction on flagpoles, values and history can see Australia emulate the "terrifying piety" of the United States. On Australia Day last year I saw the English violinist Nigel Kennedy perform at Sydney Opera House. Kennedy, the punkish busker-fiddler, always keen to please his audience, arrived on stage and immediately proceeded to play "Advance Australia Fair". As he began, everyone in the concert hall rose to their feet and sang the national anthem. This could not have happened ten years ago. And it seems to suggest that the culture of Australian patriotism has shifted from one that was extremely uncomfortable with public displays of nationalism to one that is ready to embrace a more earnest, if not in fact pious, nationalism.

I also suspect we are currently witnessing the steady militarisation of our culture. The more all-consuming the Anzac myth becomes, the less public space exists for understanding the non-military aspects of Australia's history. If current trends in publishing continue, by the centenary of Anzac Day in 2015 bookshops will need to create a new shelf category – the Gallipoli section. Increasingly, Australians are encouraged to believe that the most powerful expression of their identity and values is found in the field of military endeavour, whether through the memory of the Anzacs, or the deeds of our soldiers abroad today. In the nation's primary schools, we find posters funded by the federal government that list Australian values against a silhouette of Simpson and donkey. (Simpson was magnificent, but must his donkey be forced to carry the nation's values as well?) Brendan Nelson, charged with overseeing the enlargement of Australia's military forces, recently spoke of the purchase of new tanks as something that would help to protect Australian values for the future. John Howard, ever keen to wrap himself in khaki at military parades, farewells and welcome-homes, talks of an "Australian military tradition" within which he finds the most profound expressions of Australian identity.

Inga Clendinnen writes hopefully that good history "might even dispel our chronic amnesia regarding war". She also fears that as more public money is spent on history, there is a risk that "the historian's primary responsibility will be understood to be to the present and not to the past," and that "the true purpose of Australian history will become patriotic and integrative." I could not agree more. Yet surely the current fetish for Anzac Day as a sacred hymn of national praise, often nurtured by a surge in popular military histories of questionable quality, sends worrying signals in both respects.

Rather than encouraging us not to go to war, the resurgence of Anzac Day places performance in the theatre of war at the heart of the way we see ourselves. There is always another Gallipoli waiting around the corner. Every time we accept the myth that the Australian nation was born on the beaches of Anzac

Cove, we willingly buy into the dangerous notion that a nation is only truly formed through blood sacrifice. That myth is one we should reject, not embrace.

The Prime Minister's recent Anzac Day speeches persist in peddling the myth that Gallipoli was a noble and just cause, cleverly placing Australia's current campaign in Iraq in the same proud tradition. Once incorporated into the Anzac legend, all wars become one – noble, valiant and just. Our newfound love of Anzac, adroitly fostered by Howard, only serves to work against good history and to obscure a fundamental truth. Gallipoli was a mistake, a shameless waste of British, Australian, New Zealand, French and Turkish lives. Allied forces withdrew having achieved none of their objectives. It was a bad strategic decision, just as the decision to go to war in Iraq, which has cost somewhere in the vicinity of half a million human lives, was a bad strategic decision. The most effective way to honour those who lost their lives at Anzac Cove is continually to remember the errors of political and military judgment, to resist the tendency to value action over thought, blind service over critical judgment, and innocence and naivety over informed dissent. Many of the Anzacs the Prime Minister is so keen to lionise later questioned the judgment of the politicians who sent them to Turkey.

Of course, the story of Anzac Day's resurgence should not only be understood from the top down. There appears to be a deep need on the part of many younger Australians for a shared sacred experience. A "moving" experience of what it means to be Australian. Anzac Day fills that need. But there is much work to do before we can fully explain the resurgence of Anzac Day.

Mark McKenna

James Bradley

Not long after the publication of my last novel, *The Resurrectionist*, based in part on the Burke and Hare murders and the illicit trade in bodies during the early nineteenth century, the historian Helen MacDonald published a lengthy piece in the *Weekend Australian* critiquing it, at least in part, for its "disconcerting" use of historical figures like Sir Astley Cooper and my "hazy" grasp of the intricacies of nineteenth-century medical education.

At the time I was inclined to sympathise with MacDonald. Not because I actually was hazy about the details of nineteenth-century medical education (I wasn't, I'd just simplified them in the interests of narrative economy) or because I really did feel I'd committed some kind of calumny against Sir Astley by suggesting his porter might have bought suspiciously warm and limber corpses from resurrectionists, as Robert Knox most certainly did.

Instead my sympathy was for MacDonald as a professional historian. It wasn't hard to imagine how galling it must be to be confronted with a novel set in a period you know well, particularly when that novel plays fast and loose with the facts.

But simultaneously I found it hard to feel all that repentant. Rather like Peter Carey at that festival in Brisbane, my view was I'd written a novel, albeit a novel (loosely) based on historical material. I'd never made any claims about its historical accuracy, nor, to be honest, did I really feel I'd written an "historical" novel, at least in the reductive sense in which the term is now commonly used.

Inga Clendinnen never quite falls into the trap of assuming that novelists who tackle historical subjects are drawn to those subjects purely by a desire to re-create the past, though she comes close. But the notion of historical fiction as something closer to fictional documentary than fiction in any deep sense certainly intrudes on her analysis of Kate Grenville's *The Secret River*.

This notion is a troubling one, if only because it gives surprisingly little attention to the qualities which actually make fiction live – an appreciation of the possibilities of language; the strange, mimetic power of words to grant a kind of life to the presences which inhabit the text; its capacity for transformation and metamorphosis.

But most importantly, given Clendinnen's analysis, it's a notion of historical fiction which shackles it to the historical, and to a fairly contrived notion of accuracy. A glance backwards in time makes it clear that this connection is a relatively recent one – we certainly don't demand accuracy of Dickens in *A Tale of Two Cities*, or of Eliot in *Romola*. Nor, interestingly, do we tend to demand it of cinema, or indeed of novels written overseas, or more than about two decades ago. It seems reasonable to suggest, therefore, that the historical novel is in fact a rather more various and mutable creature than Clendinnen (or indeed Mac-Donald) gives it credit for.

Of course, Clendinnen's objections to *The Secret River* run deeper than its lack of historical "accuracy", and Grenville's seemingly "opportunistic transpositions and elisions". Her objection is essentially a methodological one, centred around the question of the limits of empathy and an irritation with the "practised slither between 'this is a serious work of history' and 'judge me only on my literary art'" many novelists fall back on when called on these questions. Not unreasonably, she disputes Grenville's claims to have re-entered the moment, and to have given a sense of how it might have been.

It is hard not to agree with Clendinnen on this last. Fiction's claims to understanding, or empathy, are not greater than history's, and are certainly less reliable. A novelist who really does think they've re-entered the moment is fooling themselves, and the perhaps unfortunate remarks by Kate Grenville notwithstanding, I'm not sure many would hold to such a claim if pressed.

The boundary is, however, less clear than it might be. Since at least the 1970s, Australian literature and Australian history have operated not just in parallel but in symbiosis. Australian novelists have taken the work of Australian historians and used it to ground their fiction, from the lush and fecund landscapes of Carey's *Illywhacker* and *Oscar and Lucinda* to the realism of *The Secret River* or the wild burlesque of Peter Mews' *Bright Planet*. These novels – and the list could go on, almost forever – have been concerned less with the historical events on which they are based than with a deeper project, something which looks rather more like the mapping out of an imaginative foundation in which a new idea of the nation might be rooted.

In turn Australian historians have taken up a parallel, but interwoven task, that of drawing forth the voices which our old idea of the country had written out. These two processes, each intimately concerned with exploring the erasures and silences of Australian history, and resolving our relationship with those erasures and silences, are not opposed, but complementary, one a mapping of the real, of what was, the other a mapping of the subconscious, of the way we understand the real, and of the way we understand ourselves. This, I think, is the point that Grenville really meant to make, and I suspect David Malouf as well – that knowing the facts is one thing, even when they are illuminated by historians of the stature of Mark McKenna or Henry Reynolds or Clendinnen herself, and that incorporating them into our sense of ourselves is altogether another.

It's not surprising that Clendinnen finds the rather careless blurring of the boundary between the two by novelists (and others) so upsetting, since it is precisely this boundary she has for many years worked to define. Whether writing about the Aztecs, the Holocaust or the early months of European settlement in Australia, she is always just as focused on the practice of history itself. As with Greg Dening's writing, this fascination is rooted in an appreciation of the ethics and limits of that practice, and it is this sensitivity which lends her work its moral clarity and sensitivity.

It would be a mistake, though, to think these are not questions novelists also wrestle with. Research is always a two-edged sword for any writer. You need to know enough not to make mistakes which will disturb the illusion you are weaving, yet the more you know the harder it becomes to break free of that knowledge and to imagine the world you are writing about anew. And likewise, there are the concerns – whether misplaced or not – about one's right to appropriate or empathise with minds and individuals embedded in cultures separate from one's own.

Ultimately the focus on the question of empathy seems misguided. Novelists may succeed or fail with audiences on the basis of their capacity to delight, but in the act of writing their real obligation is to the work, not the reader, and it is to follow the work where it needs to go, to unravel it and reveal it. As Carey argued to his audience in Brisbane, we believe or do not believe a work of fiction on the basis of the quality of the author's literary craft and powers of imagination, not because the work's characters do or do not meet narrow (and frequently contemporary) conceptions of what the past was really like. Each novel makes its own rules, and it is to these that the writer must be faithful, not to external notions of fidelity to the truth.

I don't want to suggest there aren't ethical questions writers need to work through when writing fiction. There are, but in the end the attempt to found art in ethics will always fail – the imagination is inherently transgressive and uncontrollable, and the role of good writing is not to improve us or to educate us but to live, confront, amaze, beguile.

Moving beneath both Grenville's claims for her novel and Clendinnen's and MacDonald's unease with the ways in which fiction represents the past is something else, which none of them ever quite brings into view. Why, one might ask, does Grenville feel the need to make any claim about the capacity of the novel to transcend history, while simultaneously justifying her novel by reference to historical fact? Why not just present it as a novel, and speak about the history in parallel, or as a source of inspiration?

The answer, I suspect, is that all are responding in different ways to a deeper anxiety about the nature and purpose of fiction, an anxiety which is expressed in an unease about exactly where its claims to authority are founded.

This anxiety is probably most evident in the realm of historical fiction, simply because it is there that the line is blurriest between the notion of fiction as ultimately an aesthetic creation and the documentary origins of the detail it is wrought from. But it is an anxiety that increasingly afflicts all fiction. What is it for? How do we judge it? How do we make sense of it?

Even a generation ago these questions would have been easier to answer. But we have allowed ourselves to let go of the idea that good writing – writing which bears meaning, writing which lives – is special, and an end in itself. Instead we look to the documentary and the factual to justify the imaginative aspects of fiction. And in so doing we make research the thing that matters about fiction, mistaking information for imagination, simulation for mimesis.

The reasons for this are many, and complex. Marketing must bear some of the responsibility. A novel distinguished by the strength of its writing and penetrating gaze is hard to sell to newspaper editors and media outlets; a novel based on colourful experience or real events has a hook which makes it considerably easier to sell. The way English is taught in high schools and universities, its emphasis upon themes and what would once have been called rhetoric in place of close reading, probably has quite a lot to do with it too, as does the broader retreat from the idea of aesthetic quality as founded in something deeper than personal preference.

But the emphasis upon marketing and changing educational practices are themselves only symptoms of a much larger shift in our culture, one not unconnected to the loss of the past Eric Hobsbawm describes in *The Age of Extremes*, and the onslaught of commercial trivia and self-justification Clendinnen refers to. The qualities fiction develops in readers — imagination, sympathy, a sense of the scale and complexity of human possibility — are precisely the qualities Clendinnen sees as central to the practice of history. And they are qualities increasingly at odds with the culture of instant gratification which underpins consumer society.

In such a context fiction's cultural authority and claims to the prerogative of the imagination are in a state of steady, and presumably permanent, decline. Clendinnen's analysis of *The Secret River* is one reflection of this decline, but the anxiety about the historical accuracy of fiction, and the tendency to justify it by its relationship to the real, is another. Either way it is fiction that suffers, as much as, if not more than, history.

James Bradley

Response to
Correspondence

Inga Clendinnen

I agree with everything Anna Clark has to say, especially that history, including in the schools, ought be "done", not "learnt". That means a focus on the primary materials. I was persuaded this can be done at any school level when I met a primary-school teacher from Tasmania at the recent History Summit. He has set his students to researching the histories of their families and their region, largely by way of the internet, not by accessing pre-potted information but from the documentation already available on the web, and which is constantly being augmented by the labours of archivists, museumologists and historians. Of course the students need help from time to time, but they are on a shared research adventure, and he is there to help.

I also identify, effortlessly, with Clark's Year 12 Darwin student: "Australian history just makes me want to cry. It's so boring, and I can't stand it." I felt much the same way for more than five decades, I think because at my primary school "history" was "taught" by being read aloud, chapter by dreary chapter, some-times by students and sometimes by a teacher, from a single inexorable text-book. It was not a problematic narrative: a few blackfellas, a few explorers getting lost, gold-hungry characters coming and some of them staying, "Federa-tion" – except I doubt I ever made it to Federation. That flat narrative, lacking mad monks, bonfires, kings, revolutions, golden masks, imperial adventures, had none of the overt drama of the history of France, or England, or Russia, or China, or Greece, or Italy in the flower of the Renaissance. As soon as I could choose, I chose.

Yet over the last few years I have been happily immersed in the study of the early days of contact in Australia because of the sheer richness of the written documentation, all of it written from one side of the encounter, but so rich it is possible to find real individual people lurking there. (Barangaroo has just had a slice of the Darling Harbour foreshore named after her. This gives me great pleasure.) Watkin Tench is a gift to any teacher with a touch of dramatic flair, because there he is, brimming with anecdotes and reflections, funny, and giving an enthralling account of the day-to-day affairs of a little colony teetering on the edge of starvation. Tench could be supplemented from any one of a dozen written and painted accounts, and there are great contemporary maps drawn by individuals we have come to know as individuals. There are useful compendia of daily extracts from the early journals, my favourite being Jack Egan's *Buried Alive* (Allen & Unwin, 1999).

As for the native people the British met on the beaches around the harbour – a people who at first responded to the intruders with uncanny goodwill – their traditional way of life is a study of ingenuity triumphing over circumstance. How to impart an understanding of that? I think primary school is where children are the most alert to and curious about their physical environments. I would like them to be taken on a long excursion into the bush (I'd let them keep their clothes and sunhats, I'd bring their lunch) and then given plenty of time to poke around. Then they would be asked to consider how they would go about surviving under these unpromising circumstances. Children are ingenious. I think they'd spot some of the possibilities. After that bush experience our child-friendly museums would make exciting sense to them: "So that's how they did it!" That is how Australian Aborigines managed to live in what Jared Diamond has called "the driest, flattest, most infertile, most climatically unpredictable and biologically most impoverished continent", sustaining "the least numerous human population". I would like them to be able to answer the genuinely perplexed questions: "Why didn't they invent the wheel? Why didn't they build decent reliable shelters? Why didn't they go naked?" The children would grasp that Aboriginal people had to travel fast, light, and in immediate response to changing seasonal conditions. They would realise that you can't carry a house; that you can't harness a kangaroo. It's true that some groups built permanent shelters where the living was reliably good, but Aboriginal people colonised the whole of this dry, unforgiving continent. This from the anthropologist Donald Thomson struggling to penetrate the Western Desert, to European eyes a nightmare of bald, shifting sand-dunes, and there discovering the Bindibu people, "who have adapted themselves to that bitter environment so that they laugh deeply and grow the fattest babies in the world". He has a photograph of himself cuddling a quite remarkably fat baby to prove it (Thomson, *Bindibu Country*, p.4). In the 1930s, H.H. Finlayson, Honorary Curator of Mammals at the South Australian Museum, would pack up tent, provisions and collecting gear to live alongside the people of the Central Desert. It rains through all of one long night; snug in his tent he sees their misery. But he sees something more: that by "evolving a capacity to endure, they have acquired something much more portable than a skin tent or a fur coat" (Finlayson, *Red Centre*, p.74).

Finlayson also marvelled at the exquisite exactitude of their knowledge. For example, he had thought the smaller desert rodents impossible to identify from their tracks. He had dissected their foot structures and found no differences. "Yet the blacks will unhesitatingly name the animal from its track, and it is very seldom that their preliminary identification is not confirmed when the animal is ultimately hauled triumphantly from its burrow" (p.78).

The island where I spend the winters has long ridges of crusted sand, and every morning there are the tracks of the creatures who have criss-crossed in the night. I can decipher one or two. Aborigines could read tracks as they ran. I wish I'd had an elementary course in tracking in Third Grade. A wallaby regularly comes to feed on the grass outside my study window, so I suppose you could regard it as semi-tame. But the slightest movement behind the glass and it is away, at speed, in any direction. And I wonder: how did they ever get a spear into that?

Some whitefellas seem to think that any celebration of Aboriginal ingenuity and adaptation somehow diminishes "the pioneer achievement". I don't agree. In April 1791, Marine Lieutenant Watkin Tench and three compatriots decided to explore the Upper Hawkesbury. Remember that these very peculiar imperialists had no elephants or horses or native bearers. They had to walk, carrying their own supplies, keeping the compass steady, counting their steps, slipping, sliding and doubtless swearing their way through truly punishing terrain. Out of this quietly heroic project came a map, with Tench's comments. What he sees is a desolation, with land ranging from "bad" to "worse". From the eminence he wryly names "Tench's Prospect Mount" he looks out over "very dreadful country … the ground covered with large stones as if paved". In the whole region Tench identifies only about 200 acres of potentially cultivatable land. Yet at one of those "bad places" he also sees "frequent marks of the natives". It seems it was not "bad country" for them.

Recently I made a pilgrimage to the Wiseman's Ferry area to see how it has changed from Watkin Tench's days, and I saw the heroic labour which brought the Hawkesbury region to its present productive state, not by earth-movers and chainsaws, but by pick, shovel, axe and piling stone. I noticed that nearly all the creeks running into the great river bear the names of individual Englishmen: "Webb's Creek", "Wiseman's Creek". The history of Aboriginal dispossession is written in those names. And I saw the caves hidden in what looked at first glance to be solid walls of sandstone. I didn't see the rock carvings, but I knew they were there.

Why not cultivate that binocular vision in the schools? I'd even leave the explorers in the curriculum, not because they were heroes, although some of them were, but because I would want the students to investigate precisely why some lived and others died. The layered history of this land is the surest ground for our sense of national uniqueness.

As for our later history – true, we have had no revolutions. When Phillip was struggling to sustain his miserable little convict colony on the edge of the world, events in France were drenched with drama – popular revolts, a king imprisoned, then beheaded, along with a lot of other people including some of the leading revolutionaries. Yet thirty years later, where were the principles of 1789 – liberty, equality, fraternity – most securely established? In bloodstained France? Or in that once-struggling convict colony? A social and a political miracle was wrought here, and we should understand the how of it. And, of course, the costs of it.

My ultimate hope is that through the practice in schools of the critical scrutiny of sources – the ruthless questioning of their likely reliability – will bring students to a critical, conscious scrutiny of their own responses and thinking. Achieving self-insight is a slow business. The doing of history helps it along.

Alan Atkinson asks why I did not explore "the current complex, often fertile but often acrimonious relationship between scholarship and journalism". I can't quarrel with journalists (here I am speaking of serious investigative journalists, not traffickers in opinion) because I am grateful to them. I rely on them, along with academic analysts of the contemporary world, to make my present world intelligible: to explain what is happening in Iraq or Korea or in the anterooms to the Oval Office. They also remind me that, given that present situations are so very complicated and change so swift, past situations were probably more complicated and dynamic than the serene vision of some historians would allow. Journalists' work methods look similar to ours, although it's true they work much faster. Sometimes they can look like historians on speed. One of the pleasures of the *Quarterly Essay* has been to see the hound-dog tenacity with which good journalists – Paul McGeough, Margaret Simons – pursue the "story" they are after: their swift evaluation of sources, their eager responsiveness to an inflexion. Of course hindsight has its advantages, but so does present sight. Like archaeologists, like the anthropologists, I see journalists as our kissing cousins. They stand on our side of the ravine.

Atkinson thinks I yield too much to the fictioneers in saying that historians can't "do" conversations, citing library shelves of what he calls "recorded dialogue from the past – trial proceedings, parliamentary debates, question-and-answer evidence before official inquiries" to demonstrate it. His intervention makes me remember the colloquial vigour of, for example, the Putney Debates, so I stand corrected. In fact I'm sympathetic to all his criticisms. I think that struggling to decipher the papery whispers from the past is not only a "part of the job ... worth the effort", but the most important part of the job (see my reverence for E.P. Thompson). My interest in the essay was to emphasise how austere historians must be in the business of "animating" the past. That remarkable parliament at Putney gave us authentic glimpses of informal interactions. But how many parliaments exhibit that intensity of impassioned colloquial exchange? And we still will not know how John Lilburne spoke to his daughter at breakfast. Legal records, with their elisions and standardised formulations, also stand at a distance from the urgent happenings and the urgent talk which generated and accompanied them.

A friend of mine is working on witchcraft trials in seventeenth-century France. He wants to know how the peasants of his particular region thought about witchcraft, and whether their thinking changed through time. There are witchcraft trials enough; there are verbatim records. He knows what was said in court. He wants to know how those witness and defendant statements were generated, and also what these people meant by what they said. Were they moved by old malice, new fears and angers, the cumulative force of gossip? Were they coerced by the novel and intimidating circumstance of interrogation before a panel of lofty visiting judges into formulating ideas not previously formulated? By hard labour and harder thinking he has arrived at some notion of the nature and even the sequence of the talk in a particular village tavern where some of the most serious accusations seem to have been generated. He has uncovered a small pile of strange, suggestive epithets used to describe witches, and has seen how they come to cluster fatally around particular names at particular times. I think he has learnt to "hear" his people, which is the addictive experience every historian yearns for. But he could not produce a single interchange from those testimonies and responsibly claim it to be as it had been spoken.

My own first book, *Ambivalent Conquests*, was about a catastrophe visited on the Maya Indians of Yucatan by previously nurturing Franciscan missionary friars. The friars had come to believe that their apparently meek neophytes were secret backsliders who now added blasphemy and heresy to traditional idolatry and human sacrifice. I had a mass of records as to what the Franciscans thought they were doing in Yucatan. I had the immaculate records kept by the friars of what Indians said under torture, and later what the friars said on their own behalf after there had been complaints to the Crown. I had the detailed complaints from some high-ranking Indians who had been tortured, and from outraged Spanish settlers who had tried and failed to intervene. Out of this rich trove (the Spanish colonial bureaucracy might have been slothful in action, but it knew how to look after its papers), I managed to retrieve the likely sequence of topics of conversations between accused Indians still waiting interrogation, and those brought back from the interrogators bleeding, burnt, and some with dislocated bones. I think I can hear their voices. But I cannot know the pace, the style, the intimate idioms they used among themselves in this time of stress – the kind of talk I hear whenever Jane Austen lets me eavesdrop on the conversation swirling around the Bennett family dinner table. Historians have to accept there will be limits to the access we can achieve, in contrast to the free-wheeling inventions of fiction writers.

As for History and The Market – I think the hope of much expansion of the popular market for serious history is a fantasy. This comment from a long-term survivor of the academic history-publishing trade in the United States:

> I don't buy into the problem of the decline of a non-professional audience for history. Taking a very long view – back to Livy and Tacitus – the non-professional audience has always been an elite audience. For a hundred years or so it has been a much larger elite and at times it seemed as though knowledge and learning would fall down like Portia's gentle rain, watering the meek and the strong. Then we got television … That has done a number on the illusion of the liberating potential of learning, as well as the dream of democratic good taste.

So says the voice of experience. I think he's being a touch too cynical. A lot of "historical television" is awful, but some is seriously good. Many people will read Kate Grenville's novel and be moved to think afresh about our past. I think historians have to go on writing for our dream audience, assuming their readiness to be excited by our slow, cautious explorations into the past.

What puzzles me is why novelists want to be historians at all. Some of the skills and some of the excitements might be shared, but others are different. In the September 2006 edition of the *Australian Book Review*, Gillian Dooley has a lovely essay on J.M. Coetzee and how he dealt with the flak he got for not writing explicitly political novels when he was living inside apartheid South Africa. He had this to say in a public address on "The Novel Today" delivered in Capetown in 1987: "In South Africa the colonisation of the novel by the discourse of history is proceeding with alarming rapidity" because of "the intense ideological pressure of the time." He clarifies:

> No matter what it may appear to be doing, the story may not really be playing the game you call Class Conflict or the game called Male Domination or any of the other games in the games handbook. While it may certainly be possible to read the book as playing one of those games, in reading that way you may have missed something. You may have missed not just something, you may have missed everything. ("Coetzee's Freedom", *ABR*, September 2006, p.36).

If historians came across the person called "Anna Karenina" at all, it would probably be in a small news-item about a disgraced St Petersburg matron found dead under a country train. With digging around we could get more. But we could never get *Anna Karenina*. It is nonetheless my conviction that something which comes out of the surviving records properly tested – "history" – carries a force of revelation in human affairs that fiction does not. Fiction carries us deeply, effortlessly, into imagined individual subjectivities. History is the sustained attempt to penetrate the minds and experience of actual others.

Now to my old friend John Hirst. I have never doubted either his compassion, or the depth of his concern for the present condition of Aboriginal Australians. I cannot imagine him "heartless" or "indifferent" in the face of any suffering. What I don't understand, "brilliant interpreter" though I may be, are his words on paper: his argument. I puzzle over my reading of his original statement, I look at his rebuttal, and I still can't locate my misunderstanding. Why lumber himself with that crass Kipling quotation, with its implication that we – that everyone – is or are the fruit of some dark and dirty deed, which somehow removes any possible ground for sincere moral evaluation of those deeds? I live with a small guilt for having been born into so privileged a place at so privileged a time; a rather larger one that my present comfort is traceable to the dispossession of a people I admire; an even larger one that my old body is being carefully kept alive while elsewhere in the world young bodies are left to waste and rot. Does that make me soft-headed? I exist as a moral being. The contexting historical situation also exists.

As for the Spanish Inquisition – I too intended "all the words of my sentence to count". The Inquisition was a bureaucracy operating at a distance from its victims, and one of its several aims was the pursuit of racial purity. For some of its victims recantation was not an option, or not a life-preserving one.

I continue to be unable to accept Hirst's sharp differentiation between what he defines as two large-scale attacks on Aborigines, "the first which deprived them of their land and the second which deprived them of their civil rights". To begin with the second: when did Aborigines enjoy viable civil rights in this country? As for the first: Hirst claims that my "concern for moral judgment and looking at particular cases" is "leading [me] in the direction of liberal fantasy", which he identifies as "the belief that the Aborigines could have been expropriated nicely if only there had been better communication or a treaty". That sounds more like Grenville than me. Of course I don't think that "if all the settlers had decided not to be killers, then the conquest could have occurred without killing," not only because the land uses of the two people proved inimical, but also because it is not conceivable that "all the settlers", given their cultural understandings, given their aspirations, could possibly have arrived at such a decision. Hirst also chides me for indulging in "moral judgment" and for "looking at particular cases". I thought I had made my impatience with glib moral judgments plain in the course of the essay – although I do think the study of history can improve our ability to predict consequences, and so to avoid gratuitous suffering, and also to extend the "natural" bounds of our compassion. I suspect our core disagreement derives from Hirst's liking for generalisations and my practice of focusing on particular cases. Particular cases are where the action is, and only a close examination of particular cases can lead us beyond a most sketchy and superficial understanding of how individual men understood their particular situations; how they responded to them; how they explained their actions to themselves.

Hirst's "hot" and "cold" blooded distinction between murders is not only unsustainable, but denies our ambition to understand why some white men casually killed Aborigines, other white men protected them, a few respected them, and some even came to understand and abide by their protocols.

It is simply not possible to be brisk in these matters: to rough-class and then to hit the "delete" button on what Tom Griffiths has called "the long, agonising history of the white conscience" shaping "the sinews of settler memory". Griffiths was exploring Judith Wright's very deliberate movement from the novel form to history: a movement over the same painful family ground but which freed her to "portray ... a frontier caught, from its very beginnings, in a web of intrigue, curiosity, violence and anxiety, a grave psychological embrace; and she shows how the tensions between history and memory, and between public and private, are ingrained in Australian frontier experience" ("Truth and Fiction: Judith Wright as historian", *ABR*, August 2006, pp.25–30).

We are a long way from guessing at likely blood-temperatures.

I read Geoffrey Bolton's opening comments with some pique. My aim is not to "share", or even to acquiesce in a particular cultural perspective, but to destabilise it by demonstrating that there are other ways of being in the world. And while I agree that the Aztecs of 500 years ago do indeed "baffle empathy", having written a rather large book on them I am not prepared to allow that their different cultural preoccupations "offer intractable challenges to both historians and novelists working in the early twenty-first century". To novelists? Yes. The only "Aztec" novels I know are disasters (very popular disasters). But historians? With enough thought, imagination and reflection we can draw closer than that. But Bolton makes an important point: empathy "works" with people within our own cultural milieu. We communicate fluently enough, at least with most people for most of the time, and it comes as a shock when we don't. But where is the boundary beyond which empathy, being culture-bound, leads to (often unrecognised) error? Then we have to bring something more analytic and intelligent to the task of understanding others. My own view is that sympathetic concern is essential, but that sympathetic identification cannot be trusted.

As for the lovely story of the Sudanese Ph.D. candidate – he's not the first historian to be deceived by a plausible fake (the "Hitler Diaries" come to mind). I think I would have urged him not to rewrite but to change the title: *The British Empire and the Necessity of Satire*. I'd place the Rottnest Island guillotine story in the same general category: a dramatised distillation of dark experience, lit by extravagance and humour.

On the issue of "mainstream" and "indigenous" epistemology: in my view the historian's task is to be tough-minded about all her sources regardless of their origin. Reverence for oral traditions has to be tempered by the considerable work now being done on memory, especially collective memory, and its psychological, social and political uses, which is an engrossing study in its own right. The same scepticism ought extend to all sources, including official written ones – especially when the recorders are culturally distanced from their subjects (see the errors made by a perplexed bureaucracy in pursuit of Kim Scott's Nyoongar family). Paul Veyne's apparently innocuous question: "Can this document [artefact, dance, story, ritual] really tell me what I think it can tell me?" lies at the heart of the whole historical enterprise. Although I would want to add: "What is it that this document might possibly tell me?"

I think Mark McKenna is too gloomy by half, underestimating not only the plasticity of Australian public rituals, but the vague, chronic scepticism of Australians. My personal anti-war account of Anzac Day is indeed rooted in early experience, when Anzac Day was sacred and Christmas meant presents. McKenna's view was shaped by the futile war in Vietnam, as mine was re-inforced. I think we're both guessing as to how young people think about war now. True, the flag seems to matter more viscerally (though less solemnly) now, but I think that might have more to do with sporting than military victories. As for the Anzac Cove ceremonies – certainly they were boisterous in 2005 – a giant screen, "entertainment" – but they were notably more sober this year (to see this, simply google "Anzac Cove 2006"). And while in 2005 more than 20,000 Australians, New Zealanders and British people came to the Cove, so did two million Turks, to honour the victory of the great Atatürk. What would that coming-together signify about the meaning of war?

As for McKenna's attendance at the spontaneous singing of "Advance Australia Fair" – I can't imagine what kind of audience an English "punkish busker-fiddler" would attract, and it's possible I would not have stood up. But I would like to know whether the audience response was devout, or an affectionate gesture to a popular performer, who (presumably) encouraged them to sing. Nor do I think "we are currently witnessing the steady militarisation of our culture." John Howard does not "wrap himself in khaki at military parades" (I think I have never seen him in a uniform). His role is that of the remorseful, respectful civil-ian father. And I like Simpson's modest little donkey being in the primary schools. I much prefer him to a war-horse. I would have thought that these days Australians are encouraged to find "the most powerful expression of their iden-tity and values" not in military endeavour, but in sport: a socially useful surro-gate form of war which is hard only on (well-rewarded) players.

As for the "meaning" of Gallipoli – I think many Australians are indeed watchful for "another Gallipoli waiting around the corner", precisely because they know Gallipoli to have been a blunder: "a shameless waste of British, Aust-ralian, New Zealand, French and Turkish lives". The painful heroism of indi-vidual Anzacs does not sanctify the cause, as individual Anzac survivors have made clear time and again, while the project itself is now generally agreed to be an ill-conceived, stupid waste – which only increases the poignancy of its cost. These days television keeps a constant account of the costs of war. We count the Iraqi dead, when we count them at all, in bundles. Recently *The Lancet* has come up with a careful estimate that 665,000 Iraqis are dead because of what the researchers call "conflict-related excess deaths". "Democracy" in Iraq comes at a very high price. Meanwhile, Jim Lehrer's careful count of young American soldiers dead – the slow procession of individual faces as confirmation of their deaths comes to hand – is having its cumulative impact. In this country we have yet to see soldiers killed in combat, but while we see the marches and the flags, on the same television screen we see parents, lovers and children clinging to their loved ones before they relinquish them into danger. It is also important that so many of our soldiers have gone abroad as peace-bringers, or peace-preservers, while our still-egalitarian mix of the young from all ethnic backgrounds means the immediate dangers of war will not easily be assigned to the children of the excluded, as I think has happened in the United States. I doubt militant jingoism would find much of a footing in Australia now.

I am grateful to the novelist James Bradley for his comradely wave from the other side of the ravine. For clarification: I do not think that "novelists who tackle historical subjects are drawn to those subjects *purely* by a desire to recreate the past." The best ones aren't recreating the past at all. They are making a work of art. I have a novelist friend who wrote a monumental historical novel on the French revolution; then several near-contemporary ones; now she has returned to a historical place and period. She researches at an impassioned pace until she finds a clue, an oddity, a turn of phrase which opens a vein for her rich imagination to feed on. Then she is off, and writing. She's not writing history, although she will use that research stuff to make the context as real as is convenient in terms of plot and character. She is out to wring our withers, and given her Jacobean imagination, I have no doubt she will.

Despite her serious historical groundwork, my friend knows she is writing a fiction: a fully made thing. Over the last few years people have been making a great play with the notion that "history" is a made thing too, and therefore somehow on a par with fiction in pursuit of that fleeing phantom "truth". Whatever the godlike stance adopted by some of our predecessors, historians nowadays admit that of course we "make" our histories. We couldn't simply dump the whole filing cupboard in your lap. But we make our histories out of the critical examination of the extant documents, whether artifactual or written, and by a sustained attempt to wrest from these fragments some degree of understanding. What we write is openly and obviously our construction, and therefore we have to answer for the detail and the solidity of the material, the penetration of the reasoning, the sophistication of the interpretation. And some issues, like drawing the exact divide between history and fiction, are durably recalcitrant. For a magnificent "historical novel" which seems to confound all my expressed convictions, see Penelope Fitzgerald's *The Blue Flower*, discussed in my recent selection of essays, *Agamemnon's Kiss*.

Such is life.

Inga Clendinnen
October 2006

Editor's note: Kate Grenville's response to *The History Question* was received as this *Quarterly Essay* was going to press. It, and Inga Clendinnen's reply, will appear in the next issue.

Alan Atkinson is an ARC professorial fellow at the University of New England and the author of *The Europeans in Australia: A History, Volume 1: The Beginning* and *Volume 2: Democracy.*

Geoffrey Bolton has been publishing works on Australian history since 1952, most recently *Edmund Barton: The One Man for the Job*, which was awarded the NSW Premier's Centenary of Federation Award in 2001.

James Bradley is the author of three novels: *Wrack*, *The Deep Field* and *The Resurrectionist.*

Anna Clark is a post-doctoral fellow at Monash University currently researching history teaching in Australia and Canada. Her book *Teaching the Nation: Politics and Pedagogy in Australian History* was published in 2006.

Inga Clendinnen is a distinguished historian of the Spanish encounters with Aztec and Maya Indians of sixteenth-century America. Her *Reading the Holocaust* was named a *New York Times* best book of the year and awarded the NSW Premier's General History Award in 1999. Clendinnen's ABC Boyer Lectures, *True Stories*, were published in 2000, as was her award-winning memoir, *Tiger's Eye*. In 2003 *Dancing with Strangers* attracted wide critical acclaim. Her latest book is *Agamemnon's Kiss: Selected Essays.*

Robyn Davidson was born in a small Queensland country town. She is the author of *Tracks*, the account of her epic journey across the Australian desert with four camels, which won the 1980 Thomas Cook Travel Book Award; a collection of essays, *Travelling Light*; a novel, *Ancestors*, which was published in 1989; and *Desert Places*, the story of her travels with Indian nomads. She is also the editor of the *Picador Book of Journeys*. Robyn Davidson was Macgeorge Fellow in October and November 2006, sponsored by the Australian Centre, University of Melbourne, and by the Victorian College of the Arts.

John Hirst teaches history at La Trobe University. His books include *Convict Society and Its Enemies*, *The Strange Birth of Colonial Democracy*, *The Sentimental Nation*, *Australia's Democracy: A Short History* and *Sense & Nonsense in Australian History.*

Mark McKenna is the author of *Looking for Blackfellas' Point: An Australian History of Place* and *This Country: A Reconciled Republic?*

Subscribe to Quarterly Essay

POST OR FAX THIS FORM TO: Quarterly Essay, Reply Paid 79448, Melbourne VIC 3000
Tel: 61 3 9654 2000 **Fax:** 61 3 9654 2290 **Email:** subscribe@blackincbooks.com

....

SUBSCRIPTIONS Receive a discount and never miss an issue. Mailed direct to your door.

1 year subscription (4 issues): $49 a year within Australia incl. GST (Institutional subs. $59).
Outside Australia $79. All prices include postage and handling.

2 year subscription (8 issues): $95 a year within Australia incl. GST (Institutional subs $115).
Outside Australia $155. All prices include postage and handling.

....

BACK ISSUES Please add $2.50 postage and handling to your order (or $8.00 for overseas orders).

- [ ] **Issue 1** ($9.95) Robert Manne *In Denial: The Stolen Generations and the Right*
- [ ] **Issue 2** ($9.95) John Birmingham *Appeasing Jakarta: Australia's Complicity in the East Timor Tragedy*
- [ ] **Issue 4** ($9.95) Don Watson *Rabbit Syndrome: Australia and America*
- [ ] **Issue 5** ($11.95) Mungo MacCallum *Girt by Sea: Australia, the Refugees and the Politics of Fear*
- [ ] **Issue 6** ($11.95) John Button *Beyond Belief: What Future for Labor?*
- [ ] **Issue 7** ($11.95) John Martinkus *Paradise Betrayed: West Papua's Struggle for Independence*
- [ ] **Issue 8** ($11.95) Amanda Lohrey *Groundswell: The Rise of the Greens*
- [ ] **Issue 10** ($12.95) Gideon Haigh *Bad Company: The Cult of the CEO*
- [ ] **Issue 11** ($12.95) Germaine Greer *Whitefella Jump Up: The Shortest Way to Nationhood*
- [ ] **Issue 12** ($12.95) David Malouf *Made in England: Australia's British Inheritance*
- [ ] **Issue 13** ($12.95) Robert Manne with David Corlett *Sending Them Home: Refugees and the New Politics of Indifference*
- [ ] **Issue 14** ($13.95) Paul McGeough *Mission Impossible: The Sheikhs, the US and the Future of Iraq*
- [ ] **Issue 15** ($13.95) Margaret Simons *Latham's World: The New Politics of the Outsiders*
- [ ] **Issue 16** ($13.95) Raimond Gaita *Breach of Trust: Truth, Morality and Politics*
- [ ] **Issue 17** ($13.95) John Hirst *'Kangaroo Court': Family Law in Australia*
- [ ] **Issue 18** ($13.95) Gail Bell *The Worried Well: The Depression Epidemic and the Medicalisation of Our Sorrows*
- [ ] **Issue 19** ($14.95) Judith Brett *Relaxed and Comfortable: The Liberal Party's Australia*
- [ ] **Issue 20** ($14.95) John Birmingham *A Time for War: Australia as a Military Power*
- [ ] **Issue 21** ($14.95) Clive Hamilton *What's Left?: The Death of Social Democracy*
- [ ] **Issue 22** ($14.95) Amanda Lohrey *Voting for Jesus: Christianity and Politics in Australia*
- [ ] **Issue 23** ($14.95) Inga Clendinnen *The History Question: Who Owns the Past?*

....

PAYMENT DETAILS I enclose a cheque/money order made out to Schwartz Publishing Pty Ltd.
Please debit my credit card (Mastercard, Visa or Bankcard accepted).

Card No.

Expiry date /   **Amount $**

Cardholder's name   **Signature**

Name

Address

Email

Subscribe online at www.quarterlyessay.com